THE Surface
Texture Bible

Surface

THE

Texture Bible

More than 800 color and texture
samples for every surface,
furnishing, and finish

Cat Martin

Harry N. Abrams, Inc., Publishers

A QUARTO BOOK

Published in 2005 by Harry N.
Abrams, Incorporated, New York.

Library of Congress Control Number:
2004115804

ISBN: 1-58479-452-6

Copyright © 2005 by Quarto Inc.

QUAR.SFT
Conceived, designed, and produced
by Quarto Publishing plc
The Old Brewery
6 Blundell Street
London N7 9BH
United Kingdom

Project Editor: Paula McMahon
Art Editor: Anna Knight
Designer: Joelle Wheelwright
Assistant Art Director: Penny Cobb
Photographers: Martin Norris,
Colin Bowling, Paul Forrester
Picture researcher: Claudia Tate
Copy editor: Carol Baker
Proofreader: Anna Amari-Parker
Indexer: Geraldine Beare

Art Director: Moira Clinch
Publisher: Piers Spence

Manufactured by Universal Graphics,
Singapore
Printed by Midas Printing International
Limited, China

10 9 8 7 6 5 4 3 2 1

Harry N. Abrams, Inc.
100 Fifth Avenue
New York, N.Y. 10011
www.abramsbooks.com

Abrams is a subsidiary of

Contents

Introduction

Whether chosen or inherited, interior surfaces cannot avoid forming an impression and asserting their impact on a space. From rare and extravagant materials consciously selected to flaunt and exhibit status to the mass-produced, unadorned simplicity of white paint, the combination of walls, floors, and ceilings create a specific identity for any room. You don't necessarily have to make a song and dance about your space because there is plenty of scope for neutral and inoffensive interiors that neither raise the pulse nor lower your bank balance in the extreme. Although uniformity does have a role, the last decade has seen an increased interest in individual expression. Fueled by the fantasy backdrops of luxury boutique hotels, extensive images of designer chic on the pages of glossy magazines, quick-fix home improvement television, and a multitude of new "design" stores, there is now a focus on the vast choice of available materials with which to transform the featureless into the fabulous.

The characteristics of any material are expressed by color, surface finish, inherent pattern, weight, warmth, and response to light. The properties influence not only how it looks, but also how it can be shaped, and how well it will perform and wear over time. Texture provides contrast—both visually and physically—as the underlayer of decoration disappears into the surface, sometimes to tantalizing effect. The same material can have many different textures: stainless steel can be brushed to a matte or highly polished, mirror-like finish; glass can be etched or kilnformed; leather can be embossed or split into tactile suede. No longer limited to industrial use, commercial materials, such as brightly colored resin or concrete, are increasingly commonplace in domestic interiors, providing seamless finishes. Tiled, precast or *in situ*, some materials speak for themselves, displaying a clear identity; others are increasingly linked to the latest trends with new products being launched every season. It's a fast changing world and the extent of choice is in a dizzying state of constant development.

The latest in technology has provided many new textural possibilities, allowing for surprising (and often humorous) combinations of materials and uses. New forms of familiar products—such as glass, stone, or wood—are now available, as are the latest in paints and papers or malleable, made-to-measure, vibrant plastics. Finishes are no longer restricted to familiar surfaces. Paper, for example, is now available as a floor finish; predominantly used for furniture, leather can now be applied to walls. Digital technology is increasingly

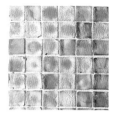

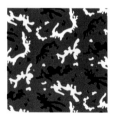

influential in the design of many finishes, and the simplest of these—paper or tiles—have been completely redefined. No longer left to chance, many finishes can now be designed to your exact specifications. Manufacturing techniques have also ensured that what was previously considered unaffordable luxury is now more readily available. Stone used to be handcrafted, but is now machine-cut and mass-produced in easy-to-use, hand-sized pieces. With purchase available over the Web, you are no longer constrained to the local supply of any given material. Location is of diminishing consequence as materials can be sourced sight unseen from all over the world.

Technology has also produced many imitation or faux materials. Artificial finishes will always enjoy varying degrees of success, but the distinction between fake and real has become increasingly blurred. Certain simulations, for instance, used to be considered second-rate and cheap, but technology has vastly improved their status. There is often no clear division between natural materials and synthetics. Some natural materials are highly processed (like linoleum), while some synthetics may have a degree of natural ingredients (like terrazzo). The term "natural" is pushed to the extreme as materials are processed beyond their original state to provide increased durability, performance, and maintenance. Artificial materials nowadays offer great natural characteristics with the joint advantages of visual consistency and enhanced performance.

The dividing line between cluttered, overdecorated interiors and unassuming, minimalist walls and floors will always be argued. Today there is huge scope for pleasure from texture as a visual and tactile experience in itself, although appearance is also affected by context and extent of application. Too much of anything may not be a good thing as it can create a clear but overwhelming identity. Even humble white paint may seem unassuming in one context, but if painted all over a room, it becomes a more elaborate and self-conscious choice. Likewise, an overabundance of stainless steel can make a space look too much like a lab; too much wood will give it a "sauna-esque" effect; and an excess of flock wallpaper will saturate a space to gravity-defying effect.

With so many finishes currently available on the market, it is impossible to go into any great detail, but *The Surface Texture Bible* does go some way to highlighting the extensive choices out there. From high-profile finishes to budget chic, it shows you some of the

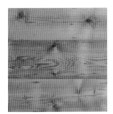

options for interesting and unusual "tactile" interiors. Bear in mind that some materials are structural and not merely decorative; there is also a degree of crossover between chapters as many materials do not fall into one category. Offering you the mundane alongside the exotic, the up-to-date and the old-fashioned, this book does not attempt to be the arbiter of taste, dictating what is hot, cold, or tepid. By including commercially available products from large multinationals, as well as local, one-off designers, it merely throws ideas into the melting pot, answers a few basic questions, and allows you to conjure up your own ideas. Some effects can be created in a weekend with a bit of home improvement, others require the specialist help of a builder, architect, or interior designer. A careful selection of hard and soft textures, for example, will create an interesting contrast of materials which will wear to varying degrees over time. There are no rules—except to consider environmental issues—and create an atmosphere which looks and feels great.

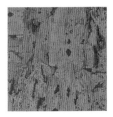

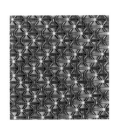

Cat Martin is a qualified architect and has been involved in a number of major commercial, public, and transportation projects, and several residential schemes for firms such as Michael Hopkins and Partners, Troughton McAslan, and Richard Rogers Partnership in the UK, and Hassell Architects in Australia. She now runs her own office, working on architectural projects, and has made freelance contributions to a number of publications and magazines, including World Architecture, Blueprint, Financial Times, Architecture Australia, Artichoke, Monument, Vogue Living, Vogue Entertaining + Travel and Condé Nast Traveller.

Carpets
& Rugs

The world of floor coverings is in
constant flux. With a huge range of
materials to choose from, carpet has
often been ignored. Today, however,
the availability of new materials,
weaves, and mixes has resulted in a
revival of this traditional form.

Aesthetics

Carpet offers unrivaled comfort and relaxation. Although less durable than other materials such as wood or stone, it has the advantages of being soft and warm to the touch, offers good soundproofing, and it won't scratch or crack. It also looks and feels warm and welcoming. In a clear break from classic cut-pile, carpet manufacturers have been busy developing an abundance of new products, mixes of materials not usually associated with carpet, and combinations of new textures and colors.

With two main types of construction—woven and tufted—different pile types are being used to create stunning new effects. There are some fabulous tactile ranges in nonuniform colors, and amazing three-dimensional piles. Comfort is definitely back on the menu, and designed to suit all budgets, so it's easy to find a cost-effective carpet solution to suit your needs.

Wool carpeting is a popular choice for the home. Despite the fact there is a limitless combination of colors and pile types to choose from (including loop, twisted, cord, cut, velvet, and shag), it is neutral naturals and beige that dominate the market. Used in classic or contemporary interiors, such carpets will survive a change of furniture or wall color, but stronger colors can breathe life into a room.

An alternative to wall-to-wall carpeting is the vast range of natural matting available today. Used as floor coverings for centuries, recent years have also seen a revival in high-quality coir, sisal, seagrass, and jute surfaces. Large expanses of floor look more interesting in a delicately textured pattern than a plain wall-to-wall carpet. The versatility of matting ensures it sits well with many types of decor. Familiar neutral shades still provide an excellent background for brightly colored rugs, but natural matting itself now comes in a selection of surprising colors, exotic patterns, and strong textures.

Rugs, low-key runners, rare kilims, Persians, and mats are some of the many soft floor finishes that need no specialist intervention—you can just throw them down yourself. Handmade or factory-woven, rugs can also be used as decoration (wall hangings) or as room dividers. Often luxurious—all-silk rugs are very soft underfoot—many are not known for their durability and so are better used purely as decoration. Some of the latest rugs have areas of block-cut pile and embossed decoration, but if you want an attention-seeking finish, then you can't beat the plush texture of shag-pile in soft yarn of mixed texture and multicolored threads.

1.1 Wool

Wool carpets are naturally hardwearing, flame-retardant, and have an inherent resistance to water, dirt, and crushing, making them suitable for use throughout the house. Available in a huge range of colors and pile, they provide a practical floor finish that is popular in both contemporary and classic interiors. The popular neutral colors will survive a change in decor, but bold colors can enhance a room.

SPECIFICATIONS

■ **Size:**
Generally 13 x 82 ft (4 x 25m) rolls, which are cut to the required length. Pile height varies. Standard tufted height is ¼ in. (6mm).

■ **Colors:**
Full spectrum. Some wools allow bettter color definition than others.

■ **Finishes:**
The wide variety of piles and weights—tufted, loop, twist, cord, cut, shag—affect appearance.

■ **Applications:**
Throughout the home, but not recommended for wet areas, such as kitchens and bathrooms.

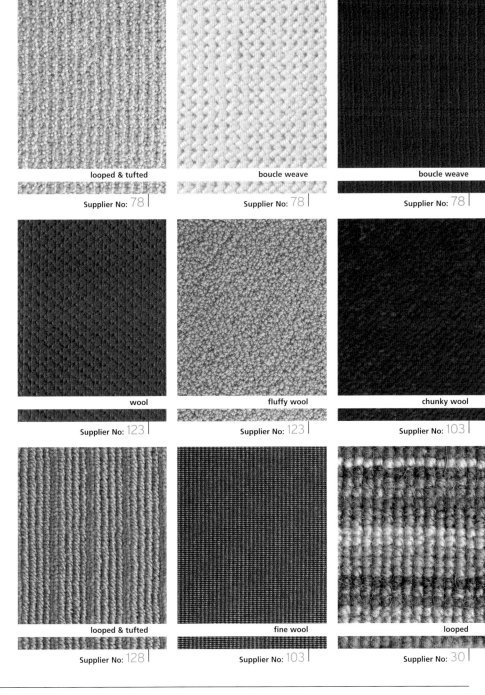

looped & tufted

Supplier No: 78

boucle weave

Supplier No: 78

boucle weave

Supplier No: 78

wool

Supplier No: 123

fluffy wool

Supplier No: 123

chunky wool

Supplier No: 103

looped & tufted

Supplier No: 128

fine wool

Supplier No: 103

looped

Supplier No: 30

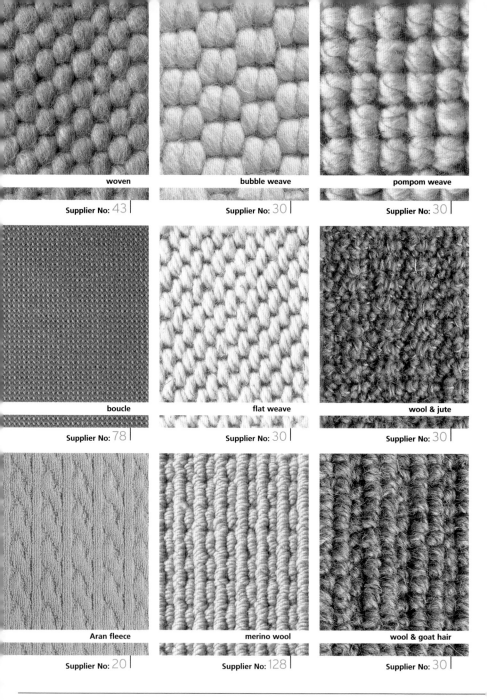

woven

Supplier No: 43

bubble weave

Supplier No: 30

pompom weave

Supplier No: 30

boucle

Supplier No: 78

flat weave

Supplier No: 30

wool & jute

Supplier No: 30

Aran fleece

Supplier No: 20

merino wool

Supplier No: 128

wool & goat hair

Supplier No: 30

tufted
Supplier No: 3

tufted
Supplier No: 30

tufted
Supplier No: 78

twisted
Supplier No: 123

line texture
Supplier No: 78

chunky
Supplier No: 103

basket weave
Supplier No: 20

looped
Supplier No: 43

looped
Supplier No: 128

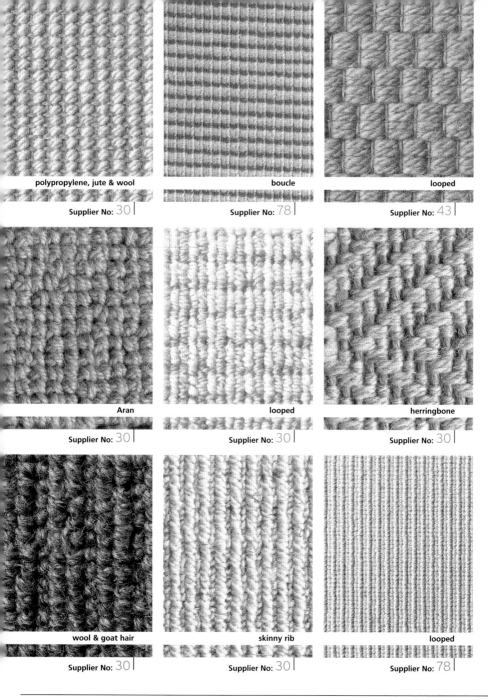

polypropylene, jute & wool

Supplier No: 30

boucle

Supplier No: 78

looped

Supplier No: 43

Aran

Supplier No: 30

looped

Supplier No: 30

herringbone

Supplier No: 30

wool & goat hair

Supplier No: 30

skinny rib

Supplier No: 30

looped

Supplier No: 78

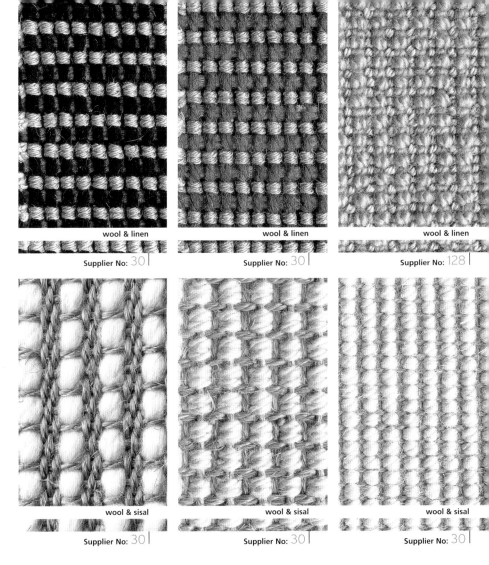

wool & linen

Supplier No: 30

wool & linen

Supplier No: 30

wool & linen

Supplier No: 128

wool & sisal

Supplier No: 30

wool & sisal

Supplier No: 30

wool & sisal

Supplier No: 30

BUYER INFORMATION

Quality is determined by the original fleece, which reacts differently to cleaning and the application of color. New fiber mixes, such as linen combined with wool, are increasingly available and cater to the luxury end of the market. Linen carpets crease easily, so use only for low-traffic areas such as bedrooms. A good-quality underlay will protect the carpet from wear-and-tear and a stain retardant can be applied for added protection. For visual consistency, manufacturers recommend the same pile weight is used throughout a domestic application.

1.2 Natural Matting

Made from renewable natural fibers sourced from around the globe, examples include sisal, coir, seagrass, abaca, and jute, offering a wide variety of textures. The neutral tones complement a variety of interiors, though use of color is growing in popularity. Affordable and durable, naturally antistatic and nonallergenic, matting provides an excellent alternative to carpeting.

SPECIFICATIONS

■ **Max size:**
Generally 13 ft (4m) wide, length is cut to the required size.

■ **Colors:**
Predominantly natural tones, but distinctive colors are available.

■ **Finishes:**
A variety of weaves and pile weights.

■ **Applications:**
Throughout the home, but not recommended for wet areas, such as kitchens and bathrooms.

colored coir

Supplier No: 102

colored coir

Supplier No: 102

colored coir

Supplier No: 102

coir herringbone, contrast

Supplier No: 30

coir rib

Supplier No: 43

coir panama

Supplier No: 30

coir herringbone

Supplier No: 30

jute boucle

Supplier No: 30

jute panama

Supplier No: 30

sisal contrast

Supplier No: 30

chunky sisal

Supplier No: 103

sisal boucle

Supplier No: 30

fine sisal

Supplier No: 103

chequered sisal

Supplier No: 103

sisal panama

Supplier No: 3

sisal panama

Supplier No: 30

sisal panama

Supplier No: 30

sisal panama contrast

Supplier No: 30

sisal boucle
Supplier No: 30

sisal boucle
Supplier No: 30

sisal herringbone
Supplier No: 30

medium sisal, colored
Supplier No: 103

sisal herringbone
Supplier No: 43

sisal
Supplier No: 30

sisal & flax
Supplier No: 103

sisal
Supplier No: 30

sisal & paper
Supplier No: 103

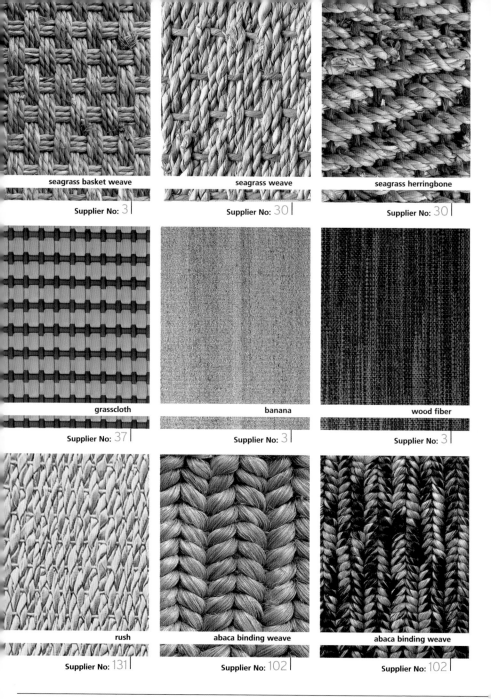

seagrass basket weave

Supplier No: 3

seagrass weave

Supplier No: 30

seagrass herringbone

Supplier No: 30

grasscloth

Supplier No: 37

banana

Supplier No: 3

wood fiber

Supplier No: 3

rush

Supplier No: 131

abaca binding weave

Supplier No: 102

abaca binding weave

Supplier No: 102

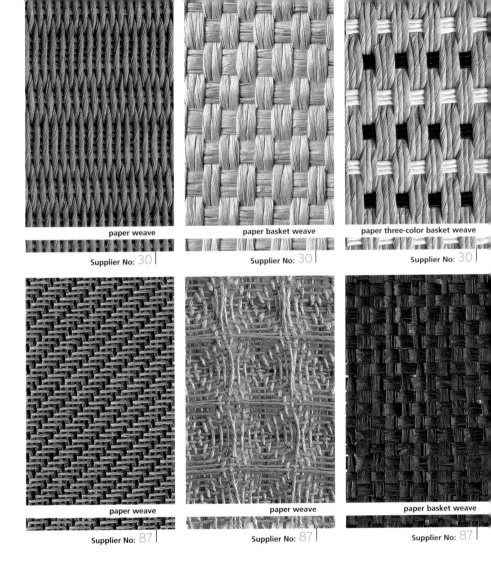

paper weave

Supplier No: 30

paper basket weave

Supplier No: 30

paper three-color basket weave

Supplier No: 30

paper weave

Supplier No: 87

paper weave

Supplier No: 87

paper basket weave

Supplier No: 87

BUYER INFORMATION

Generally good value for money, matting is relatively inexpensive and has good "green" credentials. It hides dust well, but can be difficult to clean once stained, and is not suited to kitchens or bathrooms. Matting comes in batches, so is subject to color variations and inbuilt irregularities. If lazing about on the floor is your priority, then paper flooring provides a less coarse texture, but can be slippery when wet.

1.3 Utility

The durability of a carpet depends on pile height, density, and choice of fiber. Commercial carpet technology offers a variety of tough flooring solutions suitable for heavy-traffic areas, such as hallways and stairs. Of the many types of pile available, loop-pile is generally considered the most hardwearing, but with so much variety on the market, there are plenty of tufted solutions.

SPECIFICATIONS

■ **Size:**
Generally available in tiles up to 19 x 19 in. (500 x 500mm) or widths up to 13 ft (4m).

■ **Colors:**
Full spectrum.

■ **Applications:**
General flooring for heavy-traffic areas such as hallways and stairways.

looped nylon
Supplier No: 18

cord
Supplier No: 122

synthetic
Supplier No: 83

mixed fiber
Supplier No: 20

looped nylon & wool
Supplier No: 123

striped synthetic
Supplier No: 83

BUYER INFORMATION

Nylon carpet has good antistatic properties, but a wool blend combines the best qualities of both natural and manufactured fibers for an extra heavy-wear specification. Utility carpets are generally less expensive than wool carpets. For easy maintenance and durability, carpets can be pretreated with stain and fire inhibitor. Tiles are an economical choice because wastage is greatly reduced and they can be loosely laid, making them easy to replace if damaged.

1.4 Rugs & Runners

The increase in popularity of rugs and carpets above hard flooring means there is now a huge array of textures and forms available, from traditional rugs and runners, to retro shag-piles, jumbo cords, chunky mats and deep-pile carpets, to carpets hung as room dividers or wall hangings with embossed decoration. If padding about in bare feet is your thing, then twenty-first century shag-piles offer voluminous piles in luxurious and attention-grabbing colors and weaves.

SPECIFICATIONS

■ **Max size:**
Varies greatly. Check with your supplier.

■ **Colors:**
Full spectrum.

■ **Finishes:**
Full spectrum.

■ **Options:**
A wide variety of textures and edgings.

■ **Applications:**
Runner: Stairways, hallways, corridors.
Rugs: General flooring, decorative applications.

two-tone wool
Supplier No: 121

felted wool
Supplier No: 121

felted wool
Supplier No: 121

felted wool
Supplier No: 121

wool & natural fibers
Supplier No: 121

needlepoint
Supplier No: 62

hand tufted
Supplier No: 10

contoured
Supplier No: 10

rag
Supplier No: 131

moss

Supplier No: 71

kilim

Supplier No: 43

felted wool

Supplier No: 121

leather-edged jute

Supplier No: 3

wool Venetian flatweave

Supplier No: 102

paper twine

Supplier No: 87

Tibetan wool

Supplier No: 125

felt

Supplier No: 102

cotton

Supplier No: 102

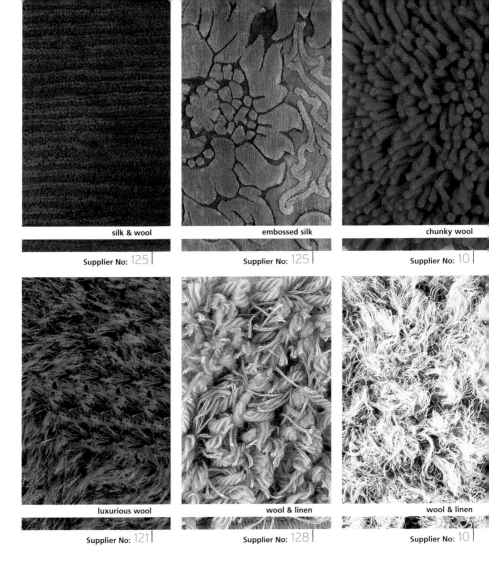

silk & wool
Supplier No: 125

embossed silk
Supplier No: 125

chunky wool
Supplier No: 10

luxurious wool
Supplier No: 121

wool & linen
Supplier No: 128

wool & linen
Supplier No: 10

BUYER INFORMATION

Highly tactile rugs in fine wool or silk provide a cushioned floor that feels great underfoot, but are made for comfort rather than durability. Runners look great on stairs or entrance halls and can often be made to order and edged with a choice of borders. Prices vary greatly depending on materials and techniques of production. The more expensive carpets are handtufted in a number of yarns for a mottled effect, which provides a subtle and sensual appeal. Bespoke rugs are available from specialist stores but can be costly.

Paint

Available in a number of finishes and colors, from understated emulsion to iridescent glazes, paint offers a mass-market and inexpensive capacity for change. Altering the color of a room is a relatively quick and economical cosmetic process that will transform and revitalize any space.

Aesthetics

Unlike many other surface finishes, paint can lift and modify the atmosphere of any room without the need for specialist help. A versatile material, it requires little in the way of equipment, and so is a popular and cost-effective option to swiftly transform any space. With a huge diversity of paints and finishes on the market, constantly changing formulations, and easy color mixing, there is seemingly endless choice. Overwhelmed by the abundance of colors available for walls, ceilings, and woodwork, many people opt for a neutral shade from one of the many "off-white" and "nearly white" paints on offer, or choose a neutral tone with a hint of color (and a rather silly name). Others choose simply to freshen up an existing color scheme. While pale colors provide an unassuming backdrop for everything else in the room, they can be rather dull. However, textural effects can be achieved using the basics: emulsion has a flat, chalky texture; eggshell is smoother, with a delicate sheen; gloss provides a fabulous contrast. Interesting effects can be created simply by painting alternating stripes of a restricted color palette on one wall.

For the more experimental, vibrant colors or metallic paint will highlight any area. The reflective properties of metallics allow for an interesting play of light. Available in pots, tubs, and sprays, these produce decorative finishes and the effect of gilding at a greatly reduced cost. However, such paints can be difficult to apply with an even tone and will appear to intensify over large areas, as well as change their appearance under different lighting conditions. Dark colors will reduce small spaces further, but the effect can be countermanded by using a lighter tone on the ceiling. Both light and dark can be used to accentuate small details or for dramatic effect. Depth and textural interest can also be created with colored wet glazes, by stippling or ragging for example, applied with brushes, sponges, and cloths. In addition, the revival of interest in "heritage" paints means a number of specialist manufacturers now blend natural pigments, sand, waxes, and minerals using traditional methods and color-matching to create paints that give an aged finish.

New technology has produced textured paints with effects such as suede and new acrylics with iridescent glazes. Environmentally friendly and low-odor paints are now available, and specialist utility paints can be tailored to specific applications, such as radiators, bathroom tiles, fridges, and kitchen cupboards. For those with a bigger budget, professionals can be called in to provide time-consuming and specialist imitation finishes— stone or marble can be recreated at a fraction of the cost of the real thing and without the inherent difficulties with installation. With a profusion of magazines and books providing step-by-step advice on colors, products, techniques, and finishes, this chapter can only hope to touch upon the myriad possibilities offered by paint.

2.1 Techniques

The best-known paint products for walls and woodwork are emulsion, gloss, and eggshell, but alternatives are available. A popular example is scumble glaze: typically milky white, it dries to a transparent delicate sheen, which can also be colored with pigments. Easily manipulated when wet, it allows a variety of different finishes (sponged, ragged, and combed).

SPECIFICATIONS

- **Size:**
Manufacturer volumes vary. Always check the coverage on the tin before buying, but a good rule of thumb is up to 475 sq. ft per US gallon or up to 70 sq. m per 5 liters.

- **Surface texture:**
Varies depending upon application.

- **Colors:**
A great choice, depending upon the manufacturer or mixing systems available.

- **Finishes:**
Generally matte, gloss, or satin, but other looks can be achieved.

- **Applications:**
Decorative finishes: walls, woodwork, furniture, floors.

stippling

Supplier No: 132

spattering

Supplier No: 132

ragging

Supplier No: 132

dry brushing

Supplier No: 132

dragging

Supplier No: 32

combing

Supplier No: 132

BUYER INFORMATION

Many paint companies now provide ready mixed color glazes and local paint suppliers can often match or create any color you ask for. A few familiar tools are all that is required, but higher-quality tools provide a better finish. Don't forget to purchase useful tools such as sponges and rags, combs, or coarse brushes, which can be used to create various effects.

2.2 Paint Effects

Historic paints are enjoying a revival and many paint manufacturers add natural pigments, dyes, waxes, sand, and minerals to their paint to create an aged finish. Traditional techniques, such as limewash and crackle glaze, are also popular. Some paints are available in premixed, rich colors, but others you will have to create yourself. A combination of paints and techniques can create truly unusual effects.

SPECIFICATIONS

- **Size:**
Manufacturer volumes vary. Always check the coverage on the tin before buying, but a good rule of thumb is up to 475 sq. ft per US gallon or up to 70 sq. m per 5 liters.

- **Surface texture:**
Varies depending upon application.

- **Colors:**
A great choice, depending upon the manufacturer or mixing systems available.

- **Finishes:**
Generally matte, gloss, or satin, but other looks can be achieved.

- **Applications:**
Decorative finishes: walls, woodwork, furniture, floors.

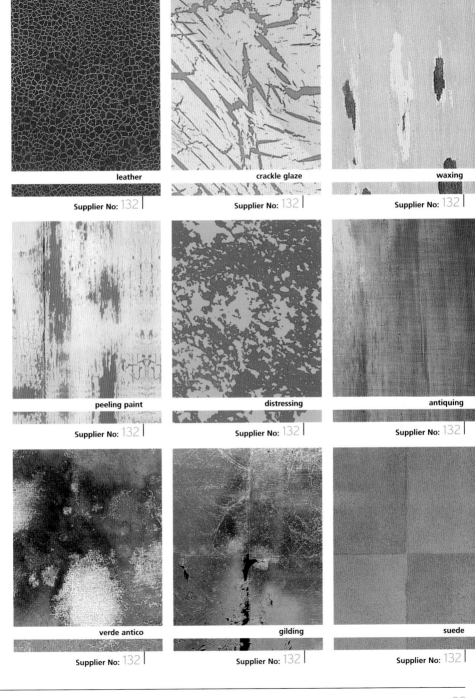

leather

Supplier No: 132

crackle glaze

Supplier No: 132

waxing

Supplier No: 132

peeling paint

Supplier No: 132

distressing

Supplier No: 132

antiquing

Supplier No: 132

verde antico

Supplier No: 132

gilding

Supplier No: 132

suede

Supplier No: 132

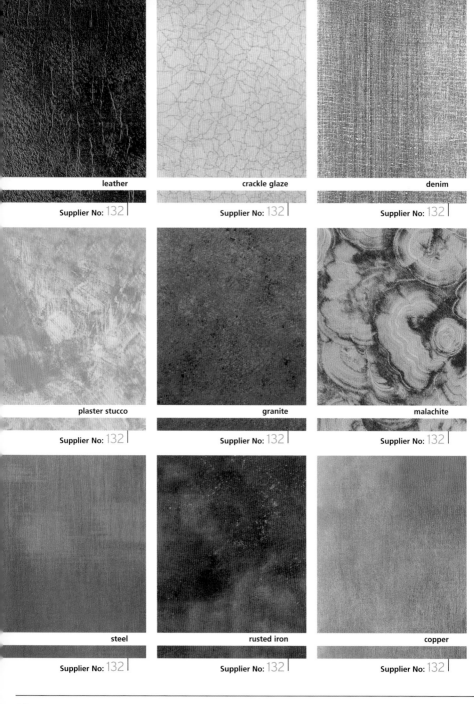

leather

Supplier No: 132

crackle glaze

Supplier No: 132

denim

Supplier No: 132

plaster stucco

Supplier No: 132

granite

Supplier No: 132

malachite

Supplier No: 132

steel

Supplier No: 132

rusted iron

Supplier No: 132

copper

Supplier No: 132

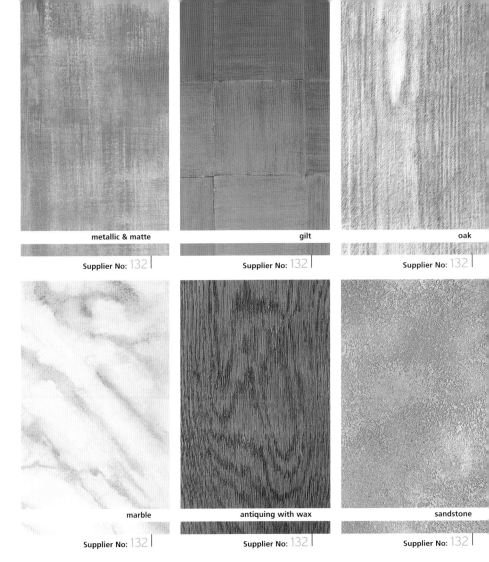

metallic & matte

Supplier No: 132

gilt

Supplier No: 132

oak

Supplier No: 132

marble

Supplier No: 132

antiquing with wax

Supplier No: 132

sandstone

Supplier No: 132

BUYER INFORMATION

Imitation finishes can be applied to a variety of surfaces and a few simple techniques can create unusual effects that plain emulsion and gloss cannot. Crackle, for example, an aged effect, can be created by layering oil and water-based paints that dry at different speeds, or by rubbing color into a topcoat of varnish. However, some effects, such as faux finishes, are more complicated and may require specialist help so do not always offer a cheap, quick, and easy transformation.

2.3 Specialist

Technological advances have meant paints are now available in almost any form, and for any purpose: metallics; tile paints, with a glossy waterproof surface; hardwearing floor paints in a range of color effects; blackboard paint for easy-wipe surfaces; fluorescents to add iridescent color to any room; even paint designed to assist uniform coverage. Or, if you prefer organic, odorless, solvent-free paints, these are available too.

SPECIFICATIONS

■ **Size:**
Manufacturer volumes vary.

■ **Surface texture:**
Depends upon application.

■ **Colors:**
A wide choice.

■ **Finishes:**
Metallic, fluorescent, sparkling, matte.

■ **Applications:**
Decorative finishes: walls, woodwork, furniture, floors. Choose the paint to suit the application.

sparkling

Supplier No: 21

fluorescent

Supplier No: 21

metalic

Supplier No: 21

crystal lacquer

Supplier No: 118

metal paint

Supplier No: 59

organic

Supplier No: 41

BUYER INFORMATION

Metallics are widely available in paint, powder, and leaf form. Translucent metallics can be used over a base emulsion to create a more subtle effect. The appearance of metallic tones will be dependent upon the presence of natural or artificial light. Use of primers and undercoats, together with quality brushes and rollers, will provide a uniform, base for the topcoat. Organic paints offer an alternative to chemical-based paints, which can cause irritation. They can be difficult to find, and some organic paints still use solvents, such as turpentine, so always check the tin before purchasing.

3 Paper

Once considered the conservative choice, recent years have seen the launch of a surprising series of innovative papers by traditional companies and newcomers alike. Developments in manufacturing techniques have allowed prints to get bigger, colors to become bolder, and paper surfaces to be manipulated into interesting textural effects.

Aesthetics

People are using paper again, but the vast number of suppliers and styles responding to demand can make the choice of papers available seem rather overwhelming. Many small design companies who are fighting for the limelight have developed specialist wall coverings, but the major manufacturers are also updating their collections with new and interesting finishes at affordable high-street prices. Even anaglypta and flock have been given a facelift, with contemporary designs in new formats that are rich and sensual to the touch. Fabrics such as silk and linen are now readily available in roll form as new techniques mean they can now be backed with paper. Less expensive—and of varying degrees of success—are those papers embossed to mimic materials, such as finely textured linen weaves, suede, and silk.

There has been a resurgence of late of all things natural, with hemp, grasscloth, cork, wood veneers, and even tea making its way onto a paper backing. Natural wall coverings conjure up an image of simple living and offer a gentle alternative to rigid patterns. Synthetic imitations of natural finishes are increasingly convincing to the eye (and the pocket). For those who prefer a more exotic look, papers can now be folded into exquisite pleats, or dusted with fine particles of mica to add sparkle—from the finest of twinkles to conspicuous disco glitter, the walls will come to life, changing color depending on surrounding lighting; whatever the choice, they will transform a room.

In a world of interactive interfaces, on paper anything is possible. Some designers have developed DIY design, with paint-by-numbers instructions and stick-on patterns that allow each wall to be custom-finished.

Developments in computer graphics have allowed those working in the field to move beyond the confines of standard print techniques while digital design has made it easy to manipulate any image to create a focus in a room, from oversized random prints, single well-chosen images, or enormous photographic montages. Paper can now be tailored to suit any interior, so there is no longer any need to search through huge collections of catalogs—instead you yourself can find your favorite image and reproduce it with relative ease. This is an opportunity to custom-design something unique—to have your own personal limited edition print—and you can now change your paper as regularly as your artwork. Modern designs are still being created using traditional handblocking methods but strictly controlled repeats are a thing of the past. Patterns are looser; contemporary designs are sharp, edgy, and more entertaining. Funky paper is the latest must-have fashion item to add drama and focus to at least one wall, and the diversity of graphic styles and matching accessories have relegated all-encompassing white surfaces to the past.

3.1 Textured

Textured wallpaper has long had an image problem. While still not considered the height of fashion, recent years have seen more contemporary designs emerge. The overstated patterns of the past are still available, but bold prints, new flock, and lightly textured papers of contrasting surfaces show there is more to wallpaper than was previously thought.

SPECIFICATIONS

■ **Size:**
Standard roll length and width depends on the manufacturer, so always check the label.

■ **Colors:**
Full spectrum. Many textured papers can be painted to suit.

■ **Finishes:**
Relief, embossed, flocked, patterned, reflective, matte, shiny.

■ **Applications:**
Full wall coverings and decorative panels.

bubble

Supplier No: 7

oval indent

Supplier No: 56

circles

Supplier No: 56

rectangle relief

Supplier No: 56

square relief

Supplier No: 56

square contrast

Supplier No: 7

crosshatch

Supplier No: 7

zigzag

Supplier No: 7

triangle

Supplier No: 56

hatched lines

Supplier No: 7

parallels

Supplier No: 56

lines

Supplier No: 61

mock weave

Supplier No: 7

herringbone

Supplier No: 7

micachip

Supplier No: 23

woodchip

Supplier No: 7

snowstorm

Supplier No: 56

waterfall

Supplier No: 56

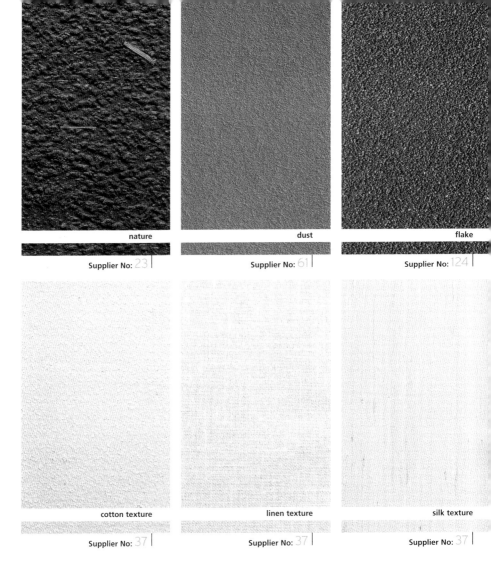

nature	dust	flake
Supplier No: 23	Supplier No: 61	Supplier No: 124

cotton texture	linen texture	silk texture
Supplier No: 37	Supplier No: 37	Supplier No: 37

BUYER INFORMATION

Papers are useful for hiding imperfections as well as being practical and long-lasting. Accurate measurements are essential when calculating the amount of paper needed for a given surface area. Allow for the pattern repeat, particularly in unusual-shaped rooms and consider the wastage involved in hanging. Papers are created in batches, so make sure you buy paper with the same batch number as variations can be minimal but are still noticeable. Some papers can be bought prepasted, which are less messy to hang.

3.2 Naturals

Natural wall coverings have been transformed from unadorned, rough textures into sophisticated and subtle papers. With natural earth tones and a pleasing unevenness in size and pattern of weave, unusual grass papers provide understated elegance, conjuring up an image of simple living, as well as a gentle alternative to rigid patterns.

SPECIFICATIONS

■ **Max size:**
Standard roll length and width depends on the manufacturer, so always check the label.

■ **Colors:**
Mostly neutral tones.

■ **Finishes:**
Texture depends on the materials used.

■ **Applications:**
General wall coverings or decorative panels.

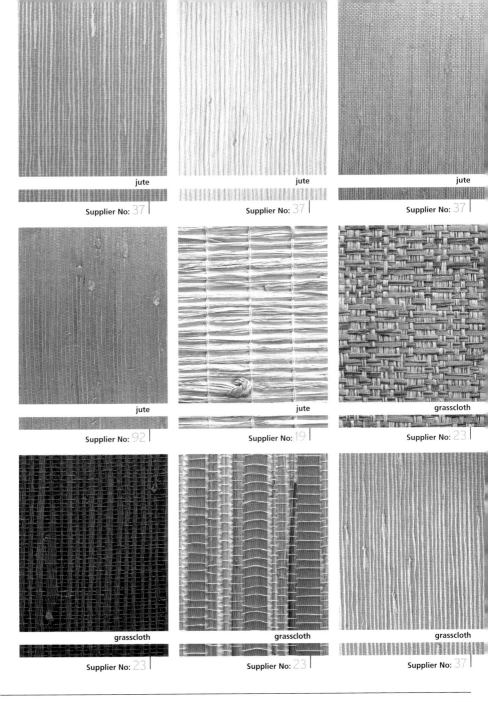

jute

Supplier No: 37

jute

Supplier No: 37

jute

Supplier No: 37

jute

Supplier No: 92

jute

Supplier No: 19

grasscloth

Supplier No: 23

grasscloth

Supplier No: 23

grasscloth

Supplier No: 23

grasscloth

Supplier No: 37

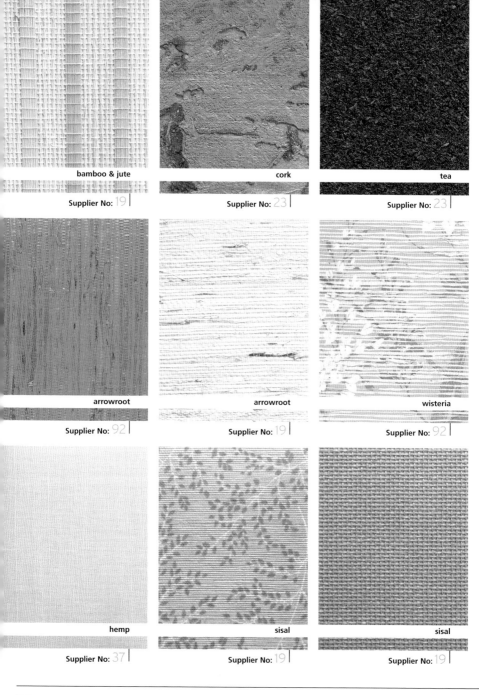

bamboo & jute

Supplier No: 19

cork

Supplier No: 23

tea

Supplier No: 23

arrowroot

Supplier No: 92

arrowroot

Supplier No: 19

wisteria

Supplier No: 92

hemp

Supplier No: 37

sisal

Supplier No: 19

sisal

Supplier No: 19

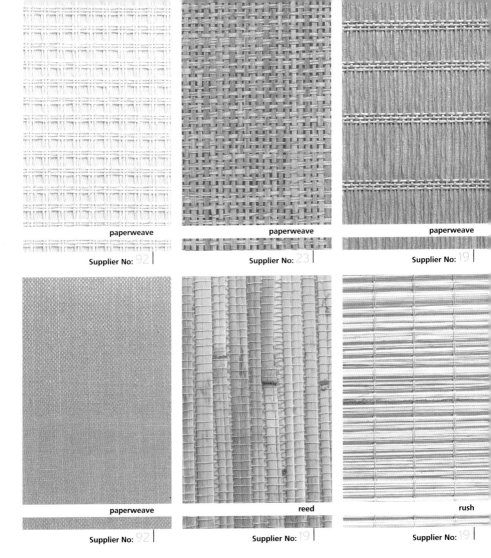

paperweave

Supplier No: 92

paperweave

Supplier No: 23

paperweave

Supplier No: 19

paperweave

Supplier No: 92

reed

Supplier No: 19

rush

Supplier No: 19

BUYER INFORMATION

Natural textures can hide imperfections well, but not all are suitable for areas of high condensation. Paper-backed rolls of delicately textured materials such as linen or silk can be found in both ordinary paper format and as framed panels. Many coverings—grasses, sand, cork, fine wood veneers, and even coverings made from tea—are now available, so there is a great deal of choice.

3.3 Special Effects

Advances in computer and print technology have altered the scale and context of traditional images by manipulating graphics to suit the buyer, offering intricately detailed images or a single graphic per panel. Other new techniques offer pleated, folded, or crushed papers—giving intricate surfaces—and metallic papers with light-reflecting qualities.

SPECIFICATIONS

■ **Max size:**
Width and length vary depending upon supplier; from standards to bespoke.

■ **Colors:**
Full spectrum.

■ **Finishes:**
Handpainted, digitally printed, pleated, folded, crushed, and metallic.

■ **Applications:**
General wall coverings and decorative panels.

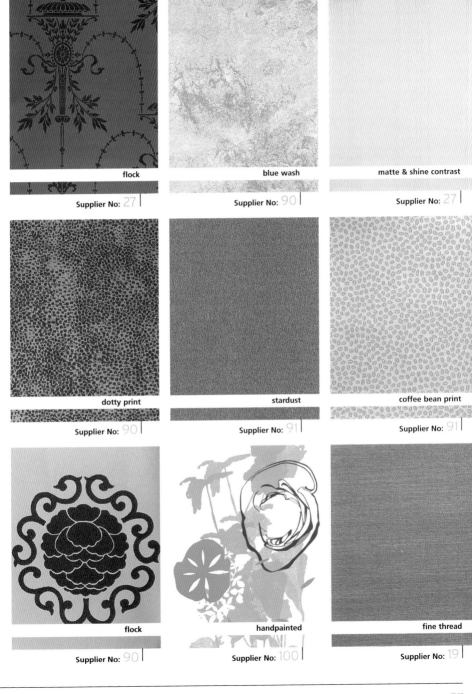

flock

Supplier No: 27

blue wash

Supplier No: 90

matte & shine contrast

Supplier No: 27

dotty print

Supplier No: 90

stardust

Supplier No: 91

coffee bean print

Supplier No: 91

flock

Supplier No: 90

handpainted

Supplier No: 100

fine thread

Supplier No: 19

pleated rice paper

Supplier No: 37

crinkled teapaper

Supplier No: 37

paper weave

Supplier No: 19

crushed paper

Supplier No: 19

folded paper

Supplier No: 124

folded metallic paper

Supplier No: 19

thread texture

Supplier No: 19

crushed paper

Supplier No: 19

paper weave

Supplier No: 19

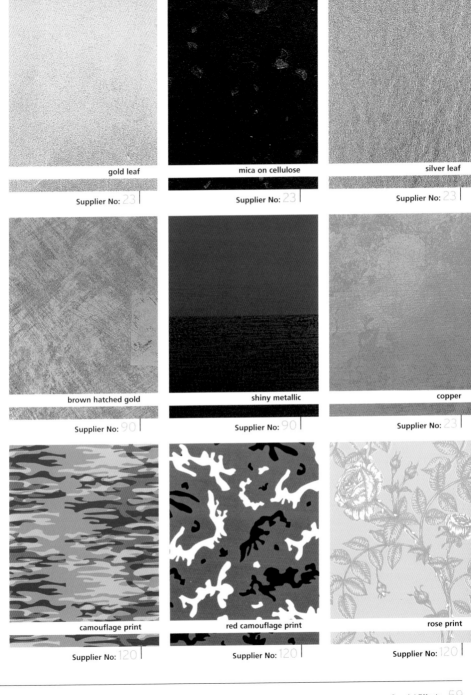

gold leaf

Supplier No: 23

mica on cellulose

Supplier No: 23

silver leaf

Supplier No: 23

brown hatched gold

Supplier No: 90

shiny metallic

Supplier No: 90

copper

Supplier No: 23

camouflage print

Supplier No: 120

red camouflage print

Supplier No: 120

rose print

Supplier No: 120

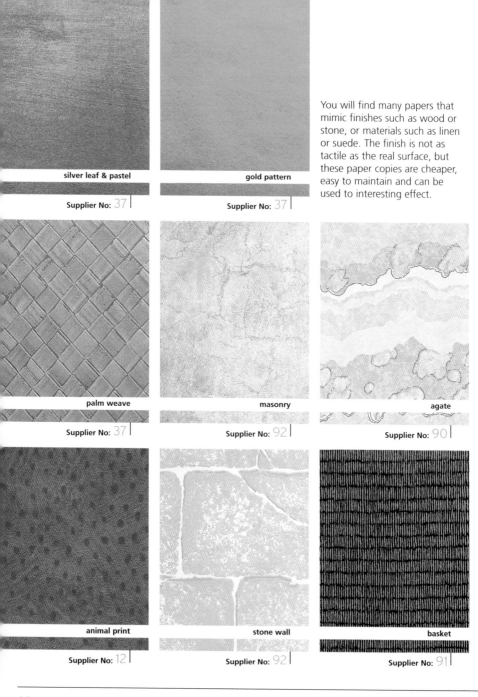

silver leaf & pastel

Supplier No: 37

gold pattern

Supplier No: 37

You will find many papers that mimic finishes such as wood or stone, or materials such as linen or suede. The finish is not as tactile as the real surface, but these paper copies are cheaper, easy to maintain and can be used to interesting effect.

palm weave

Supplier No: 37

masonry

Supplier No: 92

agate

Supplier No: 90

animal print

Supplier No: 12

stone wall

Supplier No: 92

basket

Supplier No: 91

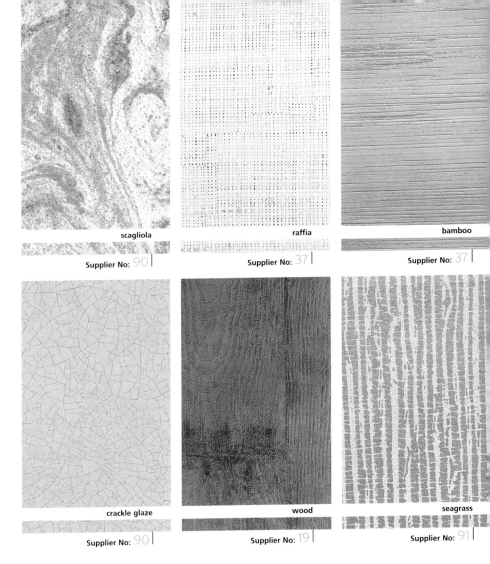

scagliola

Supplier No: 90

raffia

Supplier No: 37

bamboo

Supplier No: 37

crackle glaze

Supplier No: 90

wood

Supplier No: 19

seagrass

Supplier No: 91

BUYER INFORMATION

Any image, any size, can be printed onto a variety of papers or fabrics (although such bespoke services tend to be expensive). Some manufacturers will require a minimum order for specialized papers. When considering patterns or images, think about the number of repeats in the wall height and length.

4 Textiles

One of the most versatile aspects of interiors, designers have taken advantage of new technology to create a wealth of striking and unusual textured fabrics. Both classic and contemporary in design, they have combined fiber, color, and texture to create bold weaves, the softest silk, and eccentric jumbo felts.

Aesthetics

Perhaps more than any other group in this book, textiles have the least formal identity. Many of the other categories speak for themselves by virtue of their basic composition, but "textiles" cannot project such a distinct impression. Fabric is extremely important in helping define the character of a room, but surrounded by comprehensive collections, each with extensive ranges of fibers, styles, and colors, it's a bewildering choice. With a strong link to fashion, manufacturers are constantly updating ranges and launching new series and styles.

Textiles are incredibly versatile, particularly when driven by modern technology. As with other products, printing processes have provided new ranges, colors, and oversize prints. Machines can smooth out irregularities and manipulate the same fiber into a variety of weights and finishes: wool can become the softest cashmere, luxurious mohair, or hardy tweeds; cotton can be unusually heavy canvas or fine muslin. Recent years have seen a new playfulness enter the field with bold colors and prints, and interesting contrasts between matte and shine, translucency and opacity. The finished material can now be permanently set in a variety of textural finishes: ruched, pleated, creased, crushed, smocked, or embossed. For those seeking a more individual look, sophisticated hand-loomed textiles come in unusual and distinctive designs, each with their own unique imperfections in weave.

Despite the high turnover of styles, good-quality fabric rarely dates. The finely textured and subtle patterns of classic herringbone or woven stripes in plain neutrals (linen, cotton, or wool) will gently layer a room with unintrusive surfaces. The informal style is easy to live with, and with pattern reduced to a minimum, it will suit traditional and contemporary interiors alike. Tougher utility fabrics, such as denim or canvas, also provide an unadorned simplicity. By contrast, silk is considered a luxury. Available in a variety of weights and finishes, silk is fabulously soft to the touch, extremely lustrous, but also rather fragile.

Some materials may display an old-fashioned familiarity, but modern manufacturers add treatments that combine innovation with durability and functionalism. There is no doubt that silk adds the most exuberant shine to a surface, but don't underestimate the importance of synthetics when added to a fabric. Often scorned as cheap and nasty, modern synthetic fibers, such as acrylic, viscose, and polyester, can add interesting surface qualities, as well as practical benefits, such as resistance to stains and fire. They may change the quality and performance of a fabric, but can have surprisingly little impact on the appearance—it can be hard to distinguish a quality synthetic mix from silk simply by looking at it.

Manufacturers also provide vast ranges of coordinating papers, paints, trimmings, and accessories to add layers of comfort. Throw in too much and the result will look themed, but if restraint is used, accessories can add richness to contrast, pattern, scale, and detail. Some companies will only sell to trade, so you may need to get yourself an interior designer. If you are still unable to find the perfect textile, then some manufacturers offer a bespoke service to match specific colors and textures.

4.1 Natural & Mixed Fibers

Associated with subdued colors and a matte finish, delicate naturals like cotton, silk, and wool can provide an informal appearance for a variety of interiors. Naturals have a pleasing familiarity, and can appear raw and unrefined or formal and elegant. Technology has developed fiber mixes that produce more durable textiles for the home in a wide range of weights and finishes. Many are now available in flamboyant prints and intense colors.

SPECIFICATIONS

■ **Size:**
Standard widths depend upon manufacturer.

■ **Surface texture:**
Depends on fiber and weave.

■ **Colors:**
Full spectrum.

■ **Finishes:**
Bold patterns or a wide variety of weaves.

■ **Applications:**
Upholstery, drapes, soft furnishings, screens.

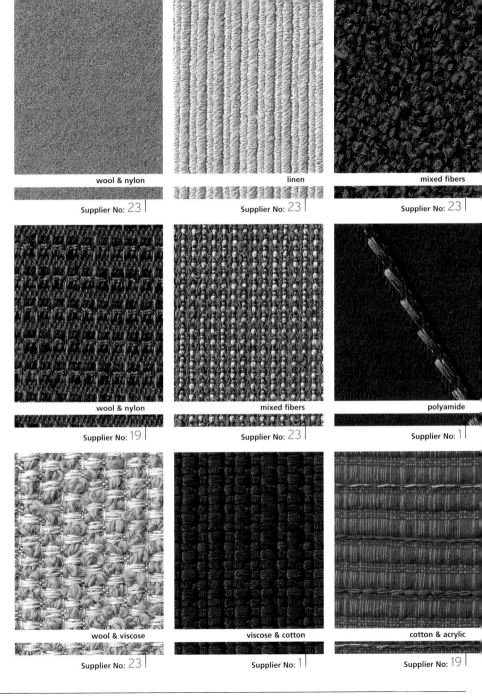

wool & nylon

Supplier No: 23

linen

Supplier No: 23

mixed fibers

Supplier No: 23

wool & nylon

Supplier No: 19

mixed fibers

Supplier No: 23

polyamide

Supplier No: 1

wool & viscose

Supplier No: 23

viscose & cotton

Supplier No: 1

cotton & acrylic

Supplier No: 19

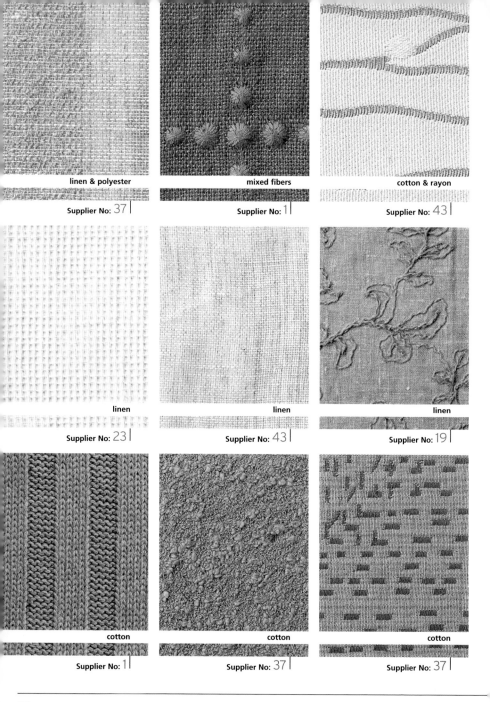

linen & polyester

Supplier No: 37

mixed fibers

Supplier No: 1

cotton & rayon

Supplier No: 43

linen

Supplier No: 23

linen

Supplier No: 43

linen

Supplier No: 19

cotton

Supplier No: 1

cotton

Supplier No: 37

cotton

Supplier No: 37

silk

Supplier No: 23

jute

Supplier No: 19

muslin

Supplier No: 15

wool

Supplier No: 84

linen

Supplier No: 102

jacquard

Supplier No: 80

BUYER INFORMATION

Technology has created mixes that can transforrn materials: cotton into linen, denim, muslin, or chenille; wool into tweed or cashmere. Silk has the softest and most subtle texture and is the most luxurious to touch, but it is also the most fragile; mixing it with cotton offers greater durability. Irregularities in natural fibers are part of their richness, but fiber mixes are generally sturdier and more durable than natural fabrics, and can be more cost-effective. If buying patterned or repeated textiles, get a good-sized sample to see how it will look before you purchase the full amount.

4.2 Utility

Utility fabrics are a good choice for upholstery as they show less wear-and-tear and are generally more durable. Modern techniques offer a range of weaves, from the traditional damasks and chenilles to the more classic herringbone or the bold colors of ripstock. Patterns can be background detail or statements in themselves.

SPECIFICATIONS

■ **Size:**
Standard widths depend upon manufacturer.

■ **Surface texture:**
Depends on fibers and weave.

■ **Colors:**
Full spectrum.

■ **Finishes:**
Bold patterns or a wide variety of weaves.

■ **Applications:**
Upholstery, wall coverings, drapes, soft furnishings, screens.

denim

Supplier No: 75

tyvek

Supplier No: 73

canvas

Supplier No: 65

ripstock

Supplier No: 131

hemp

Supplier No: 131

hessian

Supplier No: 131

BUYER INFORMATION
Fabrics are available in a wide range of colors and finishes, from classic heavy woven cottons and canvas to teflon-coated fabrics, which are extremely durable and soil-resistant. Heavy-duty fabrics are suitable wherever toughness is required. They are often resistant to tears, creasing, heat, flame, and even UV. For washable applications, ensure the fabric is washed before sewing. Seams can be sewn or glued, but some materials, such as neoprene, can be difficult to sew with regular machines.

4.3 Luxury

Modern techniques and traditional methods have combined to offer a range of tactile and luxurious fabrics—raw silk, velvets, chenilles, as well as unusual mixes, such as wool mohair and silk voile. Purchasers now have a choice between traditional but delicate fabrics, such as silk taffetas, and more hardwearing but equally glamorous synthetics.

SPECIFICATIONS

■ **Size:**
Standard widths depend upon manufacturer.

■ **Surface texture:**
Depends on fiber and weave.

■ **Colors:**
Full spectrum.

■ **Finishes:**
Bold patterns or a wide variety of weaves.

■ **Applications:**
Upholstery, drapes, soft furnishings, screens.

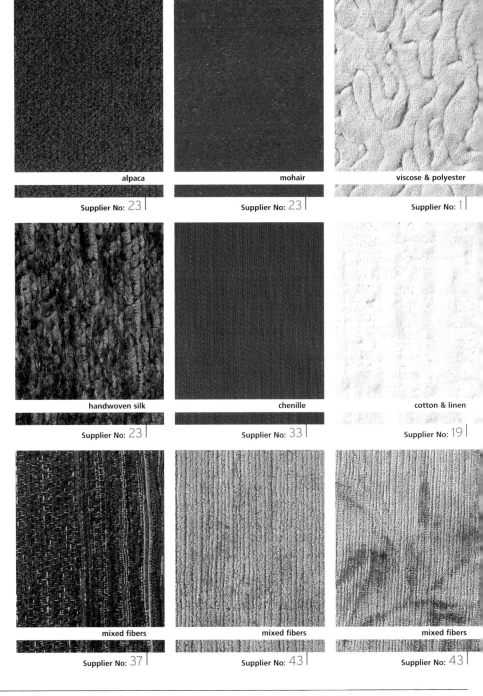

alpaca

Supplier No: 23

mohair

Supplier No: 23

viscose & polyester

Supplier No: 1

handwoven silk

Supplier No: 23

chenille

Supplier No: 33

cotton & linen

Supplier No: 19

mixed fibers

Supplier No: 37

mixed fibers

Supplier No: 43

mixed fibers

Supplier No: 43

organza silk

Supplier No: 90

sheer mesh

Supplier No: 90

chenille

Supplier No: 33

jumbo corduroy

Supplier No: 90

gold quilt

Supplier No: 15

cotton & silk

Supplier No: 48

silk

Supplier No: 90

luxurious sheer

Supplier No: 90

Ottoman

Supplier No: 80

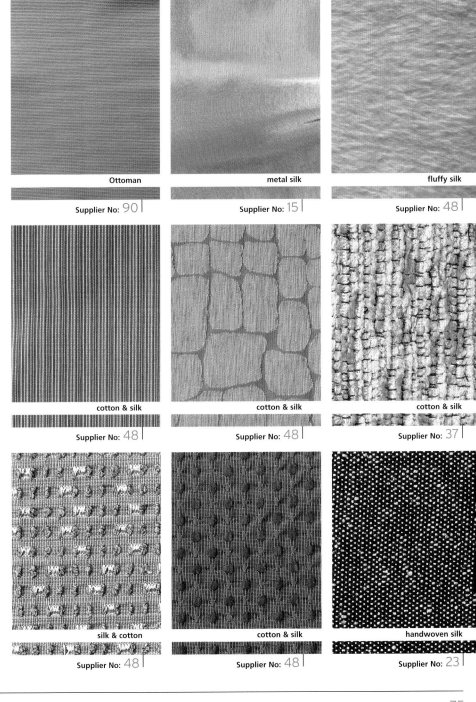

Ottoman

Supplier No: 90

metal silk

Supplier No: 15

fluffy silk

Supplier No: 48

cotton & silk

Supplier No: 48

cotton & silk

Supplier No: 48

cotton & silk

Supplier No: 37

silk & cotton

Supplier No: 48

cotton & silk

Supplier No: 48

handwoven silk

Supplier No: 23

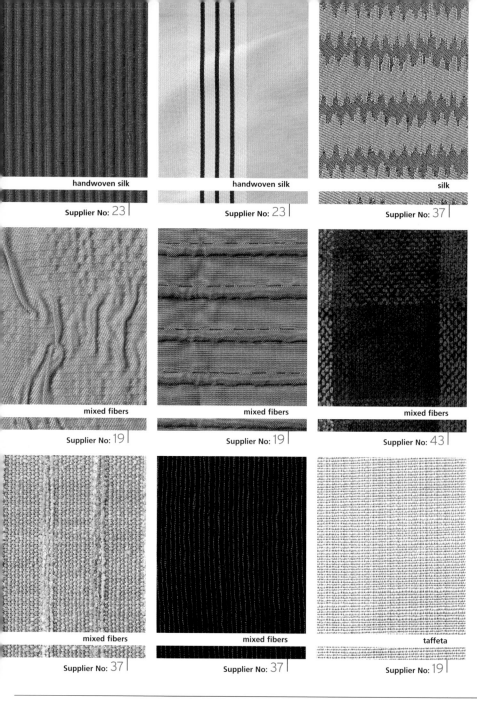

handwoven silk

Supplier No: 23

handwoven silk

Supplier No: 23

silk

Supplier No: 37

mixed fibers

Supplier No: 19

mixed fibers

Supplier No: 19

mixed fibers

Supplier No: 43

mixed fibers

Supplier No: 37

mixed fibers

Supplier No: 37

taffeta

Supplier No: 19

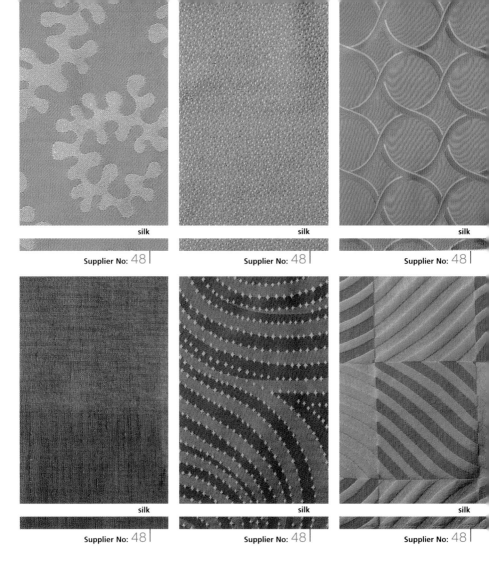

silk

Supplier No: 48

silk

Supplier No: 48

silk

Supplier No: 48

silk

Supplier No: 48

silk

Supplier No: 48

silk

Supplier No: 48

BUYER INFORMATION
Manufacturers now often provide fabric to specific requirements. They also offer complementary
wall coverings and a huge range of detailed trimmings. Handwoven cloths have fabulous
irregularities. Demand has ensured silk, velvets, and chenilles are now available at affordable
prices but manufactured blends (viscose, polyester, acrylic, and acetate) often offer equivalent
alternatives which are both cheaper and more practical.

4.4 Layers

Lace curtains were traditionally used to gently filter light while providing privacy. Contemporary materials—delicate layered organzas, lightly textured subtle sheers, and intricately detailed, laser-cut fabrics—provide the same sheer qualities, contrasting matte and shine, transparency and translucency, to add depth to any interior. Alternatively, choose chunky folds, pleats, or creased and crushed felts in bold, bright colors as hangings or room dividers.

SPECIFICATIONS

■ **Size:**
Standard widths depend upon manufacturer.

■ **Surface texture:**
Depends on fiber and weave or pattern.

■ **Colors:**
Full spectrum.

■ **Finishes:**
Translucency or solid color, woven, or textured.

■ **Applications:**
Window dressing, screens, panels, soft furnishings.

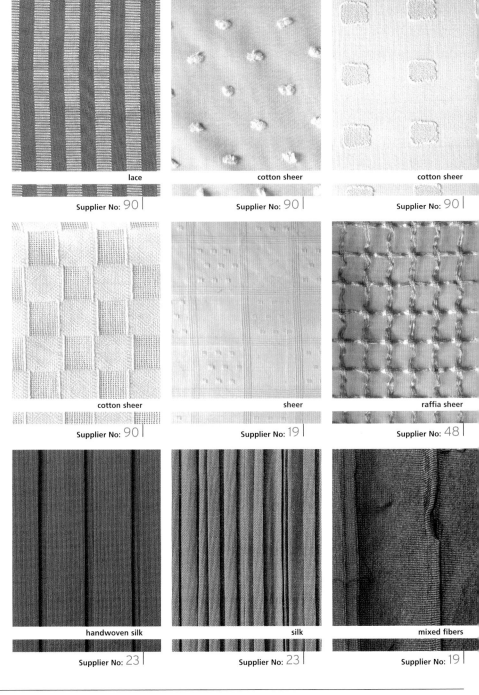

lace
Supplier No: 90

cotton sheer
Supplier No: 90

cotton sheer
Supplier No: 90

cotton sheer
Supplier No: 90

sheer
Supplier No: 19

raffia sheer
Supplier No: 48

handwoven silk
Supplier No: 23

silk
Supplier No: 23

mixed fibers
Supplier No: 19

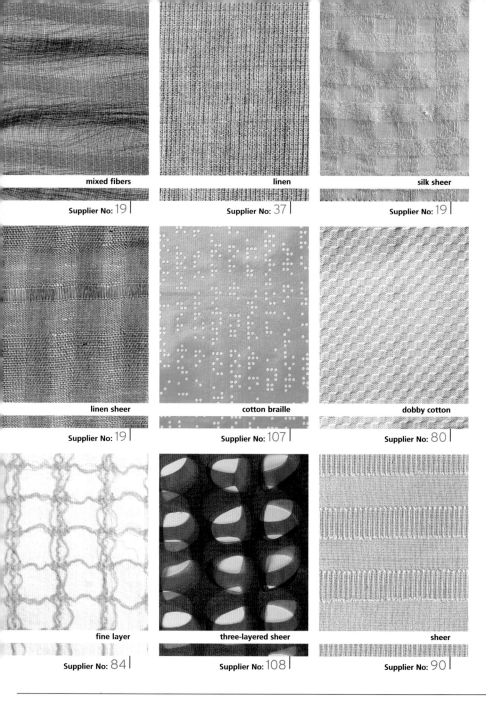

mixed fibers

Supplier No: 19

linen

Supplier No: 37

silk sheer

Supplier No: 19

linen sheer

Supplier No: 19

cotton braille

Supplier No: 107

dobby cotton

Supplier No: 80

fine layer

Supplier No: 84

three-layered sheer

Supplier No: 108

sheer

Supplier No: 90

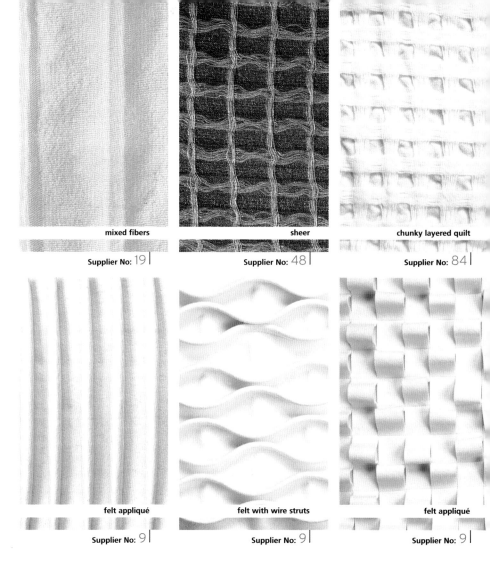

mixed fibers	**sheer**	**chunky layered quilt**
Supplier No: 19	Supplier No: 48	Supplier No: 84
felt appliqué	**felt with wire struts**	**felt appliqué**
Supplier No: 9	Supplier No: 9	Supplier No: 9

BUYER INFORMATION

Generous amounts of a less expensive material can be effective without breaking the budget. Using translucent and layed fabrics as blinds can be an economical way of covering windows if areas are measured carefully—make allowances for material shrinkage. Borders can be added to extend the fabric.

4.5 Comfort

Today there is a range of fabrics available with which to create cozy and sophisticated interiors. Soft and fluffy mixes of wool and silk can be combined with slubbed yarns and heavy weaves, or edge-stitched blankets with unusual delicate weaves, to offer an interior designed for comfort and leisure.

SPECIFICATIONS

■ **Max size:**
Standard widths depend upon manufacturer.

■ **Surface texture:**
Soft, fluffy, silky.

■ **Colors:**
Full spectrum.

■ **Applications:**
Upholstery, soft furnishings.

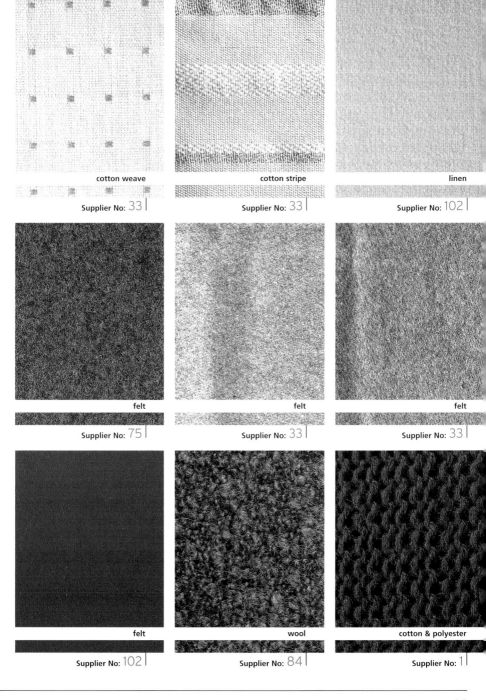

cotton weave

Supplier No: 33

cotton stripe

Supplier No: 33

linen

Supplier No: 102

felt

Supplier No: 75

felt

Supplier No: 33

felt

Supplier No: 33

felt

Supplier No: 102

wool

Supplier No: 84

cotton & polyester

Supplier No: 1

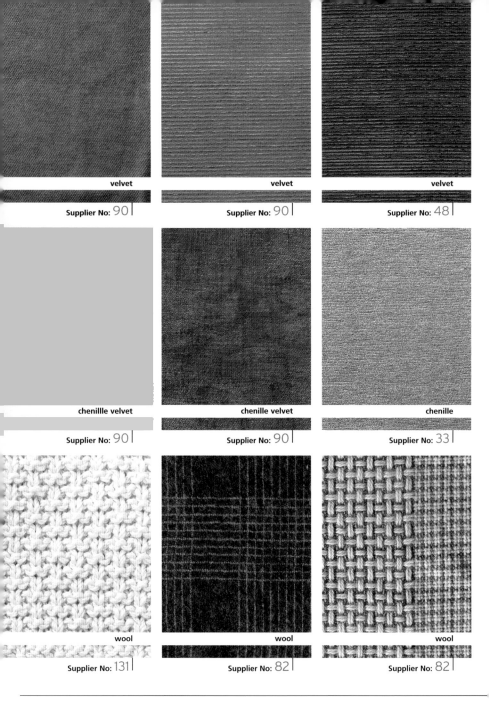

velvet

Supplier No: 90

velvet

Supplier No: 90

velvet

Supplier No: 48

chenillle velvet

Supplier No: 90

chenille velvet

Supplier No: 90

chenille

Supplier No: 33

wool

Supplier No: 131

wool

Supplier No: 82

wool

Supplier No: 82

lambswool & angora	wool	sheer wool
Supplier No: 82	Supplier No: 75	Supplier No: 48
wool	fleece	fleece
Supplier No: 75	Supplier No: 98	Supplier No: 95

BUYER INFORMATION

It is worth investing in comfortable finishing touches to areas where you spend a good deal of time. Cushions and throws can make a great deal of difference to your living area. Fabric with large patterns can be used to dramatic effect even when used for small accessories such as cushions.

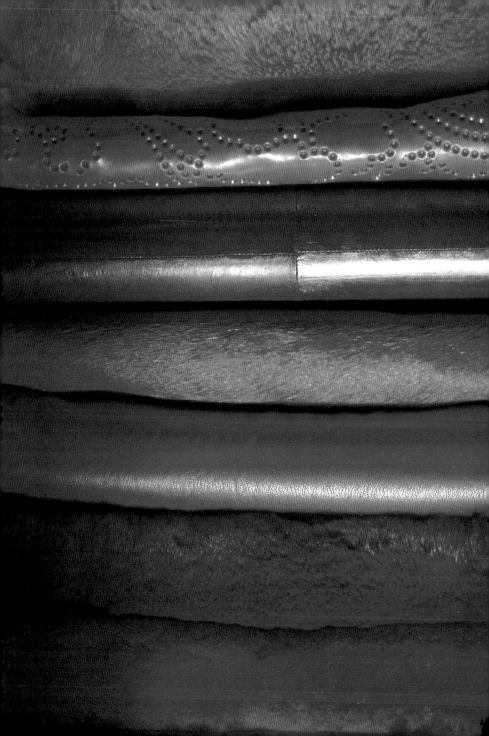

5 Leather

Used over centuries for domestic and commercial purposes, natural hides continue to appeal. Traditional and innovative processes offer countless combinations of finishes yet each skin remains unique. Fabulous to the touch, but surprisingly hardwearing, leather will add texture, contrast, and a luxurious feel to any interior.

Aesthetics

A natural and durable material, leather has a long-standing luxurious image and is enjoying a revival as a surface covering for commercial and domestic interiors. It's a diverse product, and recent years have seen an increase in the sophistication of hides and variety of applications. Leather offers a surprising range of unusual colors, finishes, and textures that work well with both traditional and modern interiors. Soft, supple, and warm to the touch, it is synonymous with luxury and is considered to be a fairly extravagant finish, but a careful choice of hide can still provide affordable sophistication. Liable to scratching and staining, as well as altering its shape after use, this merely adds to its appeal. It develops a fabulous patina and depth of character with age, improving over time and aging gracefully into elegant shabby chic. Coupled with an appealing and evocative smell, this is responsible in large part for leather's popularity.

There are many types of familiar leathers, such as buffalo, cow, bull, pig, and calf, but more exotic hides such as snake, ostrich, and pony, are also available (although generally in smaller quantities). Some skins, such as zebra, are from protected or endangered species, so be sure to source this look from the variety of convincing fakes on the market. Imitation hides tend to be more consistent, not displaying the natural flaws expected in the real thing, but have the advantage of being available in larger sheet quantities.

For a really unusual look, fish leathers are a recent success story. Using sophisticated processes, natural oils and odors are removed and the skins are softened with synthetic oils. The skins are available glazed, which flattens the scales and gives a smoother texture, or natural. Fish skins are surprisingly soft, durable, pliable, and water-resistant. The skins, including shark, stingray, perch, salmon, bass, and carp are byproducts of the fishing industry and are not from endangered species.

Perhaps best-known as a conventional upholstery material, the versatility of leather means it can be used for a wealth of alternative applications: floor finishes and wall panels, headboards, benches, curtains, shelves, log baskets, desktops, cushions, tabletops, cabinets, jewelry boxes, drawer pulls, throws, and accessories. Durable, it can also be used for tiling: surprisingly resilient and able to absorb sound, leather floor tiles can be combined with underfloor heating to provide the ultimate luxury floor finish; or it can be laser-cut to intricate detail or woven into delicate sheets. Some manufacturers offer a bespoke design service, so one-off commissions can be upholstered to suit existing interiors.

For most applications, the hair is removed during the early stages of the tanning process. Each hide will display unique qualities and can be processed to a variety of finishes. Light- or heavy-weight, leather can be soft and natural or be processed into a high-performance material, and also have a series of decorative finishes applied. Hides can also be made to resemble other skins and finishes: for example, calfskin can be transformed into a mock croc design, or pleated to resemble paper.

5.1 Hair-on-hide

Hair-on-hide skins provide luxury and warmth, adding texture across a variety of scales, from rugs to throws and wall hangings. With a great depth of finish, hides work particularly well as a contrast to more restrained surfaces, such as concrete or stone. Developments in technology mean traditional finishes like sheepskin and longhaired fleeces are now available in an assortment of striking colors.

SPECIFICATIONS

■ **Size:**
Depends on the animal.

■ **Surface texture:**
Soft, smooth, fluffy.

■ **Colors:**
Many to choose from.

■ **Finishes:**
Range from short hair to soft, fluffy, long hair.

■ **Applications:**
Rugs, throws, wall hangings, cushions.

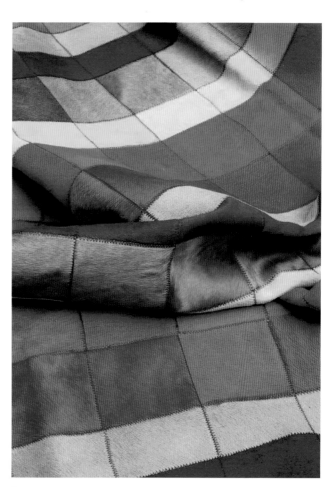

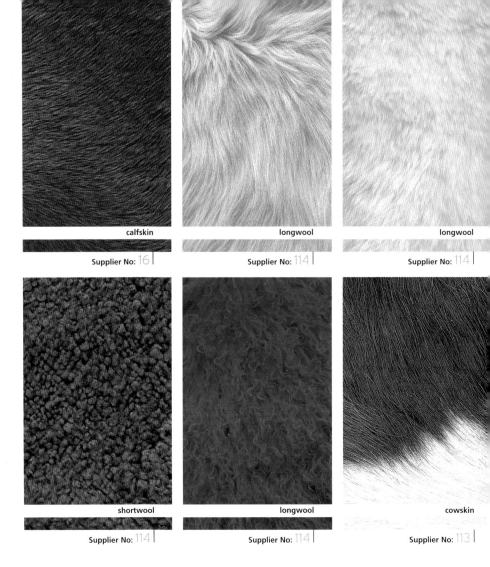

calfskin	longwool	longwool
Supplier No: 16	Supplier No: 114	Supplier No: 114
shortwool	longwool	cowskin
Supplier No: 114	Supplier No: 114	Supplier No: 113

BUYER INFORMATION

Skins are available as irregularly-shaped sheets or cut into tiles to create vast patchworks. Hair-on-hide is not suitable where fire resistance is an issue, because hair will burn easily. Hair can generally be dyed any color, but light colors are more difficult to achieve. Some hair-on-hide products can be washed easily at home, but others will need specialist cleaning.

5.2 Hides

Hides come in a huge variety: buffalo, cow, bull, pig, calf, and goat; suedes (pig) and nubuck (cow); plus exotics, such as snake, ostrich, and zebra; and even fish. The scale and location of the grain ensures each hide is unique, with its own variations in texture and tone. Hides provide a surprisingly practical and durable finish.

SPECIFICATIONS

■ **Size:**
Wall tiles can be irregular-shaped panels or available as parquet: sizes vary depending on supplier. Other hide products will also vary depending on the animal.

■ **Surface texture:**
Depends on the type, grain, and section of hide; different processes will give different surfaces. Patina will change with time and wear.

■ **Colors:**
Huge variety; added pigments create unusual colors, but white is difficult.

■ **Finishes:**
Waxed or buffed (this darkens the color); play between highly polished and matte.

■ **Applications:**
Flooring and wall cladding, upholstery, accessories.

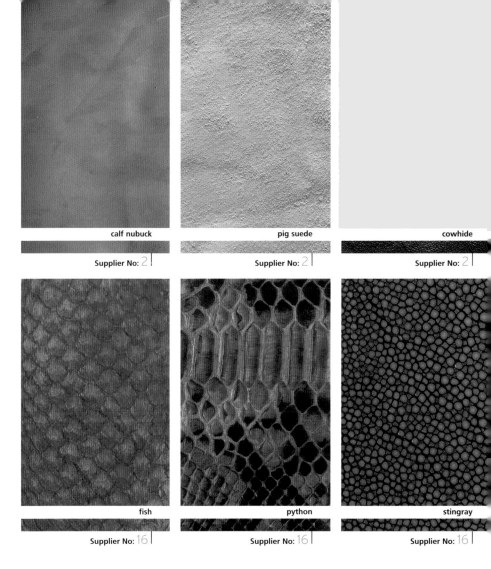

calf nubuck

Supplier No: 2

pig suede

Supplier No: 2

cowhide

Supplier No: 2

fish

Supplier No: 16

python

Supplier No: 16

stingray

Supplier No: 16

BUYER INFORMATION

There are huge differences in the handle and feel of animal leather. The toughest part is usually the central section of the hide; it is useful for more robust finishes, such as floors and walls, usually in the form of tiles. Stains and scratches are inevitable on most applications, but regular maintenance will develop an interesting patina. Spills and marks can be wiped clean or blended into the surface so leather provides a surprisingly practical finish. However, it is not a great choice for wet areas such as bathrooms. More recent developments, such as fish skin, are available only in small pieces, depending on the size of the fish, but the leather is as strong as animal leather and is just as easy to work with.

5.3 Finishes

The selected hide undergoes a series of tanning and finishing processes involving mechanical and chemical treatments, which combined with developments in color and printing techniques, shrink and dye the leather to highlight the grain and create a multitude of finishes: modern or traditional, embossed (or debossed), perforated, plated, coated, and waxed.

SPECIFICATIONS

■ **Size:**
Varies, depending on animal and product.

■ **Surface texture:**
Soft, smooth, matte, shiny.

■ **Colors:**
Full spectrum.

■ **Finishes:**
Many finishes available.

■ **Applications:**
Upholstery, rugs, panels, accessories.

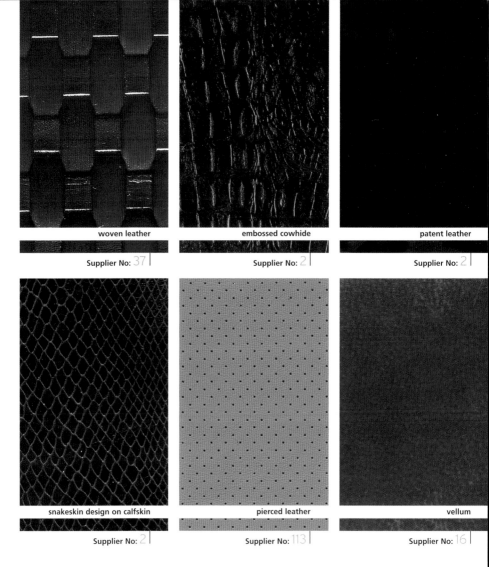

woven leather

Supplier No: 37

embossed cowhide

Supplier No: 2

patent leather

Supplier No: 2

snakeskin design on calfskin

Supplier No: 2

pierced leather

Supplier No: 113

vellum

Supplier No: 16

BUYER INFORMATION
Leather is versatile enough to be laser-cut to intricate detail or woven into delicate sheets. It can also be made to resemble other skins and finishes. It is difficult to emboss a full hide so such treatment is usually produced on half a hide. Different grades of finish will limit the final use of the hide; natural aniline leather, for example, will show marks readily whereas leather used for car seats has been chemically treated to enhance its performance.

5.4 Faux

Original materials can be imitated with varying degrees of success, and hides are no exception. The impetus behind such "fakes" is not necessarily economic but driven more by practicalities—fake suede, for example, has better stain-resistant qualities. The downside is that imitations don't possess the qualities that make real leather so appealing—patina, durability, and so on.

SPECIFICATIONS

■ **Size:**
sold by the yard (meter), widths vary.

■ **Surface texture:**
Mimics real hides, but texture can lack depth.

■ **Colors:**
Full spectrum.

■ **Finishes:**
Highly polished, matte, imitation patterns of natural hides.

■ **Applications:**
Upholstery, soft furnishings.

textured

Supplier No: 37

textured

Supplier No: 48

textured

Supplier No: 48

snakeskin

Supplier No: 14

stitch design

Supplier No: 1

weave pattern

Supplier No: 1

BUYER INFORMATION

Many manufacturers offer plain and patterned imitation leather in an array of convincing finishes and colors. Details in stitching and accessories, and subtle differences between highly polished and matte surfaces, add texture and contrast. Standard sizes make these textiles easier to work with than real hide and while there is no tactile substitute for the real thing, faux leathers offer durability and a maintenance-free finish.

6 Wood

Around for centuries, wood has always been a popular, practical, and stylish choice. More than just a basic construction material, wood is used for flooring, wall cladding, and furniture making. Manufacturers offer a wide range of finishes and patterns, available for all budgets, and applicable to contemporary and traditional homes alike.

Aesthetics

Versatile and relatively easy to manipulate, wood can be broadly divided into two groups: softwoods and hardwoods. Softwoods such as pine or spruce, are quick to grow and are relatively cheap, but wear more quickly than hardwoods. Hardwoods tend to be more expensive. Oak is one of the most diverse, and can vary enormously in color and texture.

Like other materials, wood products respond to the latest fashions and during the last decade, lighter tones such as sycamore, beech, ash, and maple were a popular choice and considered ultra chic. Recent trends have seen a shift toward darker woods, such as mahogany, walnut, and cherry, which give a richer, more traditional appearance. All types need to be finished with oil, wax, or lacquer and require periodic maintenance, but whatever your choice, wood will bring natural warmth, detail, and character to any interior.

As well as its aesthetic appeal, the durability of wood must be taken into account. All woods are fairly resilient—if maintained well—but some are more hardwearing than others. For example, maple is more robust than oak, but it is also lighter in color so can readily show scuff marks or damage. Suitable for most rooms, wood will swell with moisture, which can cause it to warp. Most manufacturers do not recommend wood for use in wet areas (such as bathrooms) unless it is properly fixed, sealed, and well maintained.

A major drawback to the use of wood in design is the ecological implications that come with deforestation. Worldwide consumption of timber is occurring faster than it can be replaced. So, if buying new wood, be sure to use an environmentally friendly source. Rare and exotic timbers, such as mahogany, teak, and iroko look stunning, but think about the environmental issues before buying. If you do want these rare woods, make sure they are supplied by an environmentally managed forest. Alternatively, reclaimed wood is extremely attractive, with an off-the-shelf timeworn patina, although finding the right quantity can be hard.

Cork is a durable and environmentally friendly option, natural in origin (although not entirely in manufacture) and available in fabulous colors and textures. Veneered wooden floors over softwood bases are cheap and quick to install, but can vary wildly in quality and finish. Processed softwood products (ply, chipboard, and MDF) are increasing in popularity among those seeking a more edgy look; and finishes, such as floor paints and stains, can be used to conceal inferior woods.

Wood may be commonplace, but that's for a reason. It's a versatile product that can be manipulated to create a number of effects, and is widely available in various formats from narrow strips or wide boards, sheets, and convincing laminates to unusual block parquets. While it needs to be cared for, it is comfortable underfoot, can be relatively economical, doesn't harbor dust, and most of all it has a lively surface and long-lasting appeal. Unlike many other materials, wood actually improves with age. Painted surfaces and carpet will eventually become scruffy with wear, but over time wood develops a rich, warm patina with a beautiful lack of uniformity and unique characteristics.

6.1 Softwoods

Softwoods include various species of pine, larch, cedar, redwood, spruce, and yew. Typically grown in colder regions (North America, Canada, Russia, Scandinavia), softwoods are from fairly rapidly growing coniferous or needle-leaved trees. Softwoods are widely used as a basic construction material, but are less durable than hardwoods. They come in a variety of precut forms and are suitable for painting or staining. More readily available than hardwoods, softwoods are the better economic option.

SPECIFICATIONS

■ **Size:**
A variety of pre-cut sizes; check with your local supplier.

■ **Surface texture:**
Depends on species, but sometimes knotty.

■ **Colors:**
Pale, golden brown, red.

■ **Finishes:**
Stained, painted, oiled, waxed.

■ **Applications:**
Interior joinery, doors, furniture, floors, wall paneling.

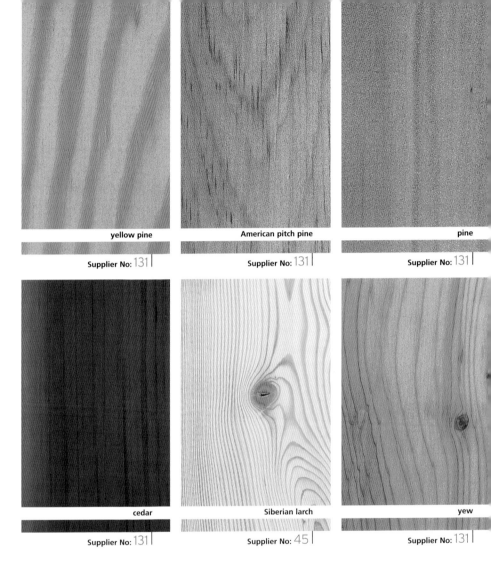

yellow pine

Supplier No: 131

American pitch pine

Supplier No: 131

pine

Supplier No: 131

cedar

Supplier No: 131

Siberian larch

Supplier No: 45

yew

Supplier No: 131

BUYER INFORMATION
If working with a restricted budget, cheaper wood, such as pine, can be stained the color of other woods, such as walnut or cherry, to create an effective but economical finish. Available in narrow strip or wider boards, molded skirting, or tongued and grooved timber panels. When purchasing timber, allow for the reduction caused by planing. Softwoods should be treated against rot and woodworm before use.

6.2 Hardwoods

Hardwoods offer an extensive range of grain, texture, and color. Grown in temperate and tropical areas, hardwoods can be deciduous or evergreen and therefore encompass a broad range of species. Light-colored woods are common in Europe and the United States, and darker woods come from more tropical climes. Enormous variations exist within each type. Some hardwoods are less readily available so can cost more.

SPECIFICATIONS

■ **Size:**
A vast array of sizes: narrow strip, solid plank, tile, block, veneered boards.

■ **Surface texture:**
Depends on species.

■ **Colors:**
Wide range of grain and colors.

■ **Finishes:**
Needs to be reapplied, many boards are pre-finished with oil, lacquer, or wax.

■ **Applications:**
Interior joinery, floors, wall paneling, doors, furniture.

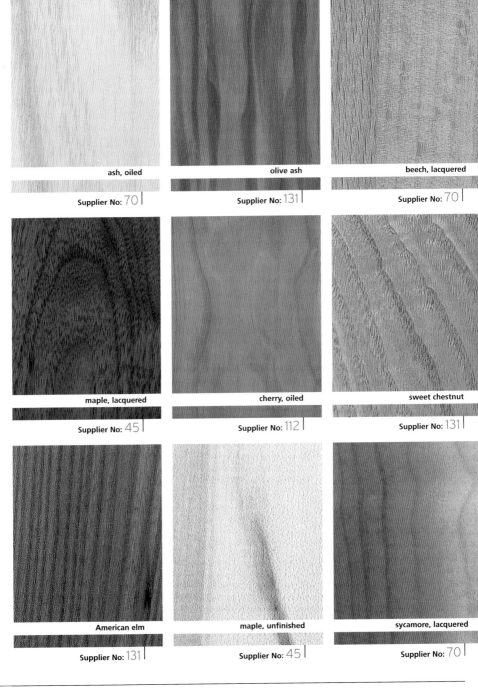

ash, oiled

Supplier No: 70

olive ash

Supplier No: 131

beech, lacquered

Supplier No: 70

maple, lacquered

Supplier No: 45

cherry, oiled

Supplier No: 112

sweet chestnut

Supplier No: 131

American elm

Supplier No: 131

maple, unfinished

Supplier No: 45

sycamore, lacquered

Supplier No: 70

red oak, oiled
Supplier No: 70

American white oak, oiled
Supplier No: 70

Europan oak, unfinished
Supplier No: 45

Norman oak, waxed
Supplier No: 45

dark oak, smoked
Supplier No: 112

oak, lacquered
Supplier No: 45

reclaimed oak
Supplier No: 112

oak, endgrain
Supplier No: 45

Surface treatments should be reapplied on a regular basis: oil provides a natural finish which is permeable but can be reapplied; lacquer entails minimal maintenance and copes with heavier traffic but wears over time; wax provides an appealing steady build up of patina and offers a traditional look, but it is high maintenance.

zebrano, unfinished

Supplier No: 45

Arura vermelho

Supplier No: 112

teak

Supplier No: 45

rosewood, lacquered

Supplier No: 45

paduak, unfinished

Supplier No: 45

sylvared, lacquered

Supplier No: 70

wenge

Supplier No: 131

coco wood

Supplier No: 70

umbra

Supplier No: 70

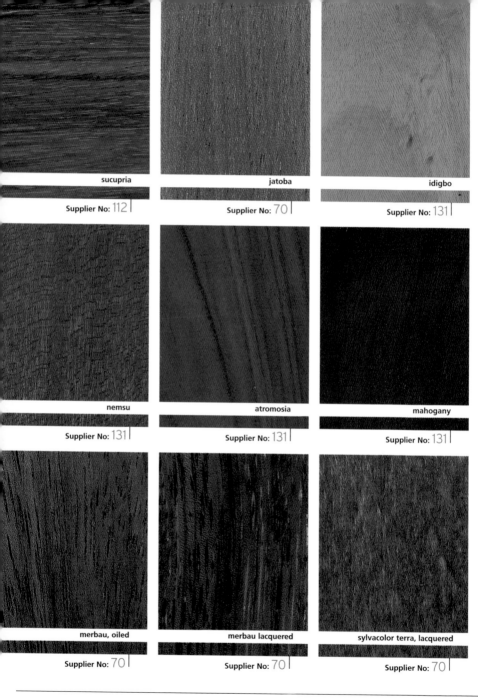

sucupria

Supplier No: 112

jatoba

Supplier No: 70

idigbo

Supplier No: 131

nemsu

Supplier No: 131

atromosia

Supplier No: 131

mahogany

Supplier No: 131

merbau, oiled

Supplier No: 70

merbau lacquered

Supplier No: 70

sylvacolor terra, lacquered

Supplier No: 70

Veneers are produced by cutting thin slices off the log, which produces subtle variations in grain and color. Various methods of cutting produce different visual characterisitcs, but maximum leaf size is limited to the size of the log. This can be an economical way of achieving a stunning effect, but ensure each leaf is related to the adjacent (bookmatched) and exposed edges (such as nosings to veneered shelves) are edged in solid wood to match.

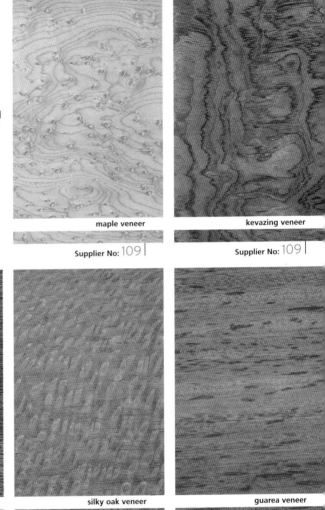

maple veneer

Supplier No: 109

kevazing veneer

Supplier No: 109

walnut, bookended veneer

Supplier No: 45

silky oak veneer

Supplier No: 109

guarea veneer

Supplier No: 109

BUYER INFORMATION

Hardwoods are admired for their strength and durability, as well as the wide range of colors and decorative effects. While sharing similar grain patterns and textures, each wood has its own distinctive characteristics. Birch is fairly weak and often used as a facing for ply. Oak is strong and versatile, and good for heavy traffic flooring, but isn't easy to work. Mahogany is durable, dense, and resists decay. Walnut has a rich color and distinctive grain but is not hardwearing.

6.3 Blocks & Parquet

There are two main timber alternatives to straight boards—parquetry and block. Small blocks or strips of timber were traditionally laid in a herringbone pattern, but a range of contemporary patterns are now available. Blocks can be arranged in any pattern. Smaller scale finishes, such as mosaic, are usually laid in preassembled small tiles.

SPECIFICATIONS

- **Size:**
Thickness varies from ¼-¾ in. (6-22mm) and lengths vary according to pattern required.

- **Surface texture:**
Mosaic, strip, and block will show natural variations in the wood.

- **Colors:**
Wide range of grain and color.

- **Finishes:**
Can be bought prefinished or unfinished, oil or wax will need to be reapplied periodically.

- **Applications:**
Flooring.

Burmese teak

Supplier No: 76

jarrah

Supplier No: 76

English oak

Supplier No: 76

Burmese teak

Supplier No: 76

oak

Supplier No: 127

Rhodesian teak

Supplier No: 45

BUYER INFORMATION

Parquet floors are typically laid in geometric designs onto a smooth, level floor. Costs vary according to choice of timber, pattern, and the preparation required. Some parquet floors can be purchased in prefabricated larger tiles, prefinished with stain retardant and a protective topcoat. This can make installation easier, but patience is still needed. Laying parquet floors can be difficult and may require specialist help.

6.4 Antique & Reclaimed

Salvaged boards avoid machined uniformity with pleasing irregular surface textures and uneven sizes. Time—and numerous applications of wax—have endowed them with an attractive patina. Of great charm, drawbacks include the need to de-nail, and possibly re-machine, before use; thus, while undoubtedly eco-friendly, they are not always the most economical choice.

SPECIFICATIONS

■ **Size:**
Depends on availability.

■ **Surface texture:**
Antique, usually a worn, interesting patina.

■ **Colors:**
Depends on wood, but woods often darken with age.

■ **Finishes:**
Wax, oil, lacquer.

■ **Applications:**
Flooring, wall paneling, interior joinery, furniture.

pine

Supplier No: 76

Canadian maple

Supplier No: 76

walnut

Supplier No: 76

cherry

Supplier No: 76

antique French oak

Supplier No: 76

Bordeaux oak

Supplier No: 76

BUYER INFORMATION
Reclaimed wood is an excellent environmental choice, but it is not always a cheap option. Salvaged from old houses, buildings, and even boats, it is available from timber salvage specialists, second-hand building material outlets and larger demolition companies. Check your local area. When considering availability, oak is a good choice. Boards are typically longer and wider than their modern counterparts; items, such as sleepers, can provide an uneven finish on a larger scale than is available with standard woods.

6.5 Decorative Finishes

Involving high levels of craftsmanship, marquetry juxtaposes different woods inlayed in complex designs. Woods are hand- or laser-cut into intricate patterns to create interesting depth and shadow effects. Laser technology and advances in wood dyes and glues mean there is a greater choice for all budgets.

SPECIFICATIONS

■ **Size:**
Marquetry varies from small items to entire walls. Other finishes can be applied to any wood.

■ **Surface texture:**
Marquetry generally produces a smooth finish. Other finishes produce a variety of textures.

■ **Colors:**
A wide variety.

■ **Finishes:**
Marquetry is usually lacquered and polished.

■ **Applications:**
Furniture, wall panels, doors, screens, ceiling roses.

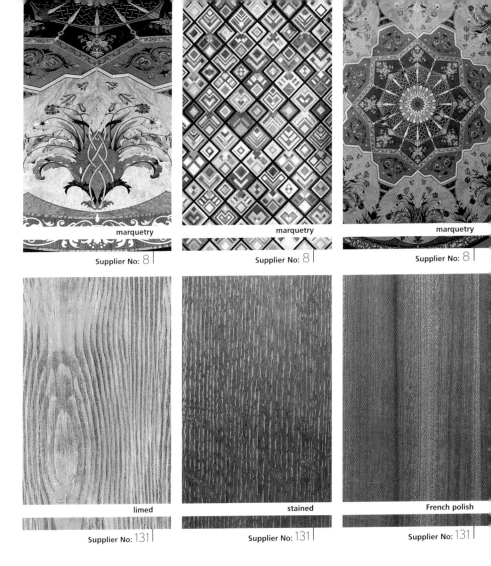

marquetry

Supplier No: 8

marquetry

Supplier No: 8

marquetry

Supplier No: 8

limed

Supplier No: 131

stained

Supplier No: 131

French polish

Supplier No: 131

BUYER INFORMATION

Marquetry is a great way to use exotic timber in an economical way, but designs are usually bespoke so can be expensive. The veneers can suffer in extreme temperatures and humidity. Less specialized decorative finishes include: staining (available solvent- and water-based), an economical decoration for cheaper woods; varnish (available in various colors); liming (wide range of colors); French polishing (a method of applying shellac); and painting (one of the most common finishes).

6.6 Processed Boards

An interesting substitute for solid wood, processed boards can be laminated, or used as finishes in their own right. They are utilitarian in look and, when pretreated, can be more resistant to changes in humidity and temperature.

SPECIFICATIONS

■ **Size:**
Each of the processed woods are produced in varying thicknesses, but come in standard sheet sizes that can be cut to suit requirements.

■ **Surface texture:**
Varies from the satin-smooth feel of birch ply to the roughness of chipboard. Hardboard has a rough side and a smooth side.

■ **Colors:**
Natural or dyed.

■ **Finishes:**
Stained, varnished, oiled, waxed, painted (brushed or sprayed).

■ **Applications:**
Floors, subfloors, shelving, doors, furniture, wall paneling.

punched hardboard
Supplier No: 126

MDF, black
Supplier No: 63

MDF, natural
Supplier No: 99

rough chipboard
Supplier No: 131

smooth chipboard
Supplier No: 131

birch plywood
Supplier No: 109

BUYER INFORMATION

Processed boards are significantly cheaper than solid wood. Available in large sheets and panels of varying strengths and compositions, they offer a difference in scale to solid timber and stripboards. Varieties include: blockboard (range of thicknesses and veneer finish), ply, MDF, chipboard, and hardboard. Chipboard is weaker than ply or blockboard and its use is decreasing as other products are now on the market. MDF is versatile and can be moisture-resistant and flame-retardant if treated. It is easy to work and to cut to clean edges, and is available in lightweight formats. For most processed woods, many companies offer a cut-to-size service, so non-standard sizes are available.

6.7 Laminates

Laminates offer an affordable substitute to solid wood flooring and are available to suit all budgets in a variety of finishes and levels of quality. Relatively quick to install and hardwearing, one drawback is that damage can be more difficult to repair than real wood floors. New gluing systems mean larger-scale laminated wall panels can now be purchased, offering great acoustic potential.

SPECIFICATIONS

■ **Size:**
Sheet and plank sizes vary depending on manufacturer.

■ **Surface texture:**
Flat or grain textured in strips or blocks.

■ **Colors:**
Extensive range of natural wood colors.

■ **Finishes:**
Prelacquered, matte, gloss.

■ **Applications:**
Flooring, wall paneling.

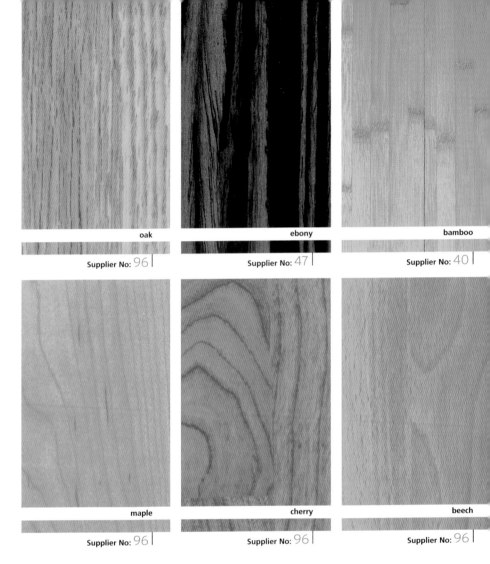

oak

Supplier No: 96

ebony

Supplier No: 47

bamboo

Supplier No: 40

maple

Supplier No: 96

cherry

Supplier No: 96

beech

Supplier No: 96

BUYER INFORMATION

Laminates are available as a thin veneer of real wood on a softwood or processed plank and as a sheet material comprised of thin layers of printed paper treated with resin and heated at high temperature to bond. Laminate floors are ideal in demanding areas such as hallways and can be installed in bathrooms where wood is more problematic. However, they can be noisier than natural wood floors. Wear-resistance varies between products, as do manufacturer guarantees. Glue-free joints allow for a quick installation and matching accessories, such as skirtings, are easily available.

6.8 Bamboo & Cane

Bamboo is a grass, but flooring is usually supplied as prefinished (lacquered) engineered boards, making it strong and suitable for heavy-duty use. Alternatively, bamboo strips can be sewn together to create rugs. Cane is a solid core material, the vines are extremely strong, light, and durable, and can be woven into a variety of furniture designs and accessories.

SPECIFICATIONS

■ **Size:**
Varies.

■ **Surface texture:**
Wide or narrow grain.

■ **Colors:**
Naturally pale to dark brown, but can be painted or stained.

■ **Finishes:**
Gloss or semi gloss.

■ **Applications:**
Wall panels, floors, furniture.

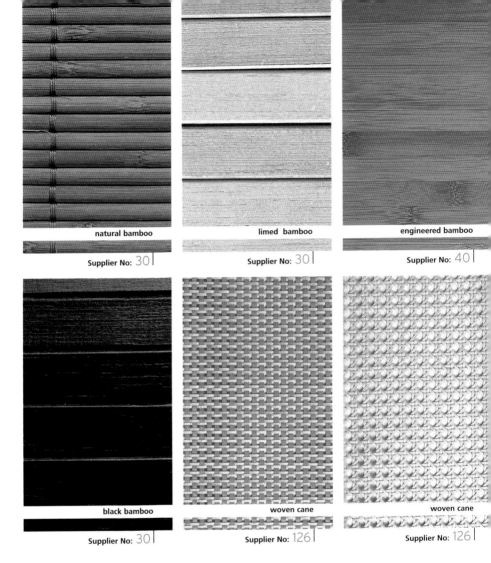

natural bamboo

Supplier No: 30

limed bamboo

Supplier No: 30

engineered bamboo

Supplier No: 40

black bamboo

Supplier No: 30

woven cane

Supplier No: 126

woven cane

Supplier No: 126

BUYER INFORMATION

Engineered bamboo boards are resistant to buckling, warping, and shrinkage, and can also tolerate moisture, making a bamboo floor an attractive and durable alternative to hardwoods. Usually sold as tongued and grooved boards, bamboo flooring is easy to install and the grain yields an interesting effect. Bamboo's rapid regenerative properties make it an ecologically sound and distinctive floor finish or wall cladding.

Typically used for furniture, cane can be creatively adapted for other areas of the interior, such as mats and blinds.

6.9 Cork

A renewable resource, cork is hardwearing with inherent antislip properties; it is also resilient and easy to maintain. Cork can be sanded and resealed if worn, and should last for decades. Warm and slightly springy underfoot, it offers excellent heat and sound insulation. It is also relatively cheap.

SPECIFICATIONS

■ **Size:**
Typically available in rolls, planks, and tiles of varying thicknesses, grades, and dimensions. Standard tile size generally 12 x 12 x ⅛ in. (300 x 300 x 3.2mm)

■ **Surface texture:**
Varying density of granules.

■ **Colors:**
Range of color-veined and natural tiles; unsealed tiles can be color-tinted with a water-based paint.

■ **Finishes:**
Waxed or varnished to varying degrees of shine (matte, satin, high gloss). Can be bought prefinished.

■ **Applications:**
Commercial or domestic; wall and floor tiles, good for bathrooms.

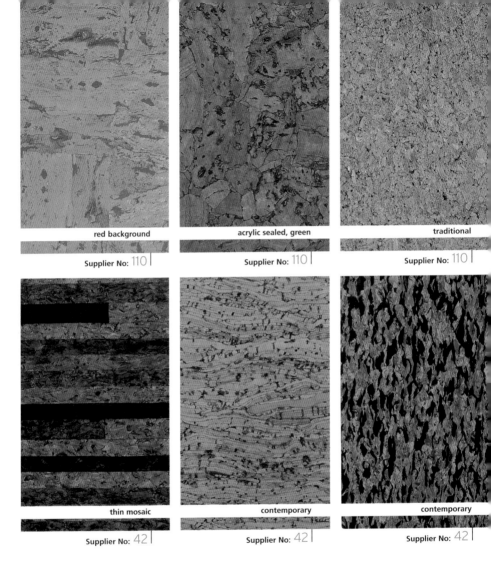

red background

Supplier No: 110

acrylic sealed, green

Supplier No: 110

traditional

Supplier No: 110

thin mosaic

Supplier No: 42

contemporary

Supplier No: 42

contemporary

Supplier No: 42

BUYER INFORMATION

Manufactured from the bark of living trees, cork is the ultimate sustainable material. Naturally hypoallergenic, antistatic, and low maintenance, cork is an ideal floor choice for residential and commercial applications. Its antislip properties make it ideal for bathrooms, but it must be sealed to make it waterproof. Presealed tiles can be purchased, but it is advisable to give it a sealing coat once laid. Cork can be applied over most existing surfaces, so less preparation is needed.

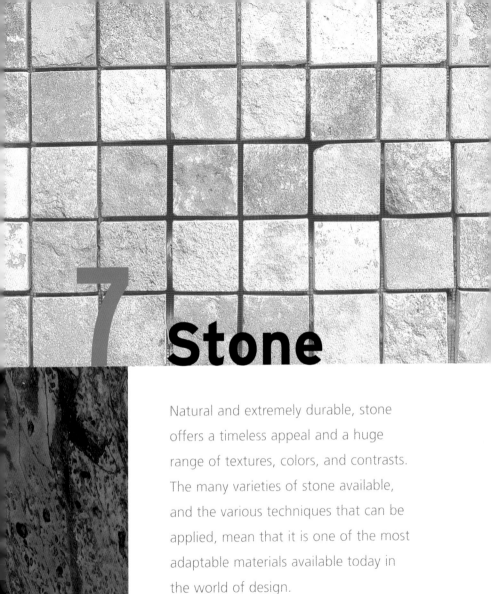

7 Stone

Natural and extremely durable, stone offers a timeless appeal and a huge range of textures, colors, and contrasts. The many varieties of stone available, and the various techniques that can be applied, mean that it is one of the most adaptable materials available today in the world of design.

Aesthetics

Stone is a versatile material that sits well alongside a variety of other finishes. The main choices for interior applications are limestone, slate, marble, and granite, but there are many varieties in between. The specific classification of stone is according to its texture and mineral composition (igneous, sedimentary, metamorphic), but as the basic constituents are preimposed by nature, man can only remove and remold. Natural stones have been quarried for centuries, but each quarry is unique so differences in texture and tone are to be expected. The following images cannot show the full richness or character of the various types of stone, and even samples are only ever intended as a guide because tonal colors will vary from batch to batch.

Stone can be used in interiors for walls, work surfaces, basins, and fireplaces, but is predominantly used for high-traffic areas, such as flooring. Hardwearing but naturally cool underfoot, stone actually retains heat well so is a good choice for use with underfloor heating. Although problems with cold feet can be resolved, the other inherent characteristic of stone is that its hardness will amplify sound.

Stone is a practical and diverse material. A designer can choose between brash and ostentatious or subtle and subdued—pale limestone can appear calm and understated; slate has an interesting lack of uniformity and a natural sheen; marble has a uniform surface and a distinctive crystalline structure which can be polished to a high gloss. As well as the aesthetic variations of background color, veining, and uniformity, the density and durability of stone should be considered when planning its place within an interior. The selected surface finish can also alter the appearance, feel, and practical qualities of a surface. The characteristics of stone determine possible surface treatments, and there are many options (only the most common are mentioned here), including matte, polished, honed, riven, antiqued, sandblasted, and smooth. Identical stones can be machine-cut and polished smooth to an immaculate seamless surface or, alternatively, "aged" in a process called "tumbling" which reveals the beauty of the stone and gives the impression of many years of use. Choice of finish all depends on what appearance you are trying to achieve.

Also influential when considering appearance is the scale of the stone. Quarried stone historically was laboriously hand-cut, but modern technology has allowed us to manipulate blocks into precision-cut slabs, sheets, tiles, and mosaics, of a variety of sizes and thicknesses to suit a range of applications. The availability of the thinner, uniform-cut tiles has increased the range of finishes to choose from. Maximum slab sizes vary from stone to stone, but larger items such as worktops generally can be tailored to suit customer requirements.

Stone is natural, versatile, and extremely hardwearing. It will never be the economical option to purchase or install, but new technology means stone such as marble, previously considered an unaffordable luxury, is now more reasonably priced, and some stones naturally offer a cheaper option than others. Installed correctly and with a little periodic maintenance, it provides an elegant and tactile surface that should be a practical investment for any interior.

7.1 Limestone

Limestone comes in a number of varieties, ranging from extremely porous to very dense. It can be split (cleaved), sawn, or cut before a wide variety of different surface finishes are applied. Traditionally subtle in coloring, it is also available in an assortment of striking colors, making it suitable for both classic or modern interiors.

SPECIFICATIONS

■ **Size:**
Tiles are usually square, but sizes vary depending on supplier.

■ **Surface texture:**
Fine to medium-grain, often speckled with random shell flecks.

■ **Colors:**
Buff tones to pure white, blue gray; purest limestone is white.

■ **Finish:**
Honed, polished, antique, flamed.

■ **Applications:**
Facing stone, tiles, setts, fireplaces, floors, paving, skirting.

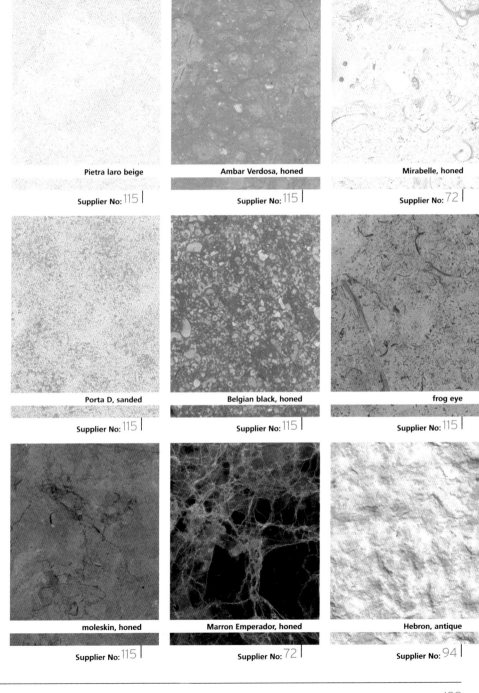

Pietra laro beige

Supplier No: 115

Ambar Verdosa, honed

Supplier No: 115

Mirabelle, honed

Supplier No: 72

Porta D, sanded

Supplier No: 115

Belgian black, honed

Supplier No: 115

frog eye

Supplier No: 115

moleskin, honed

Supplier No: 115

Marron Emperador, honed

Supplier No: 72

Hebron, antique

Supplier No: 94

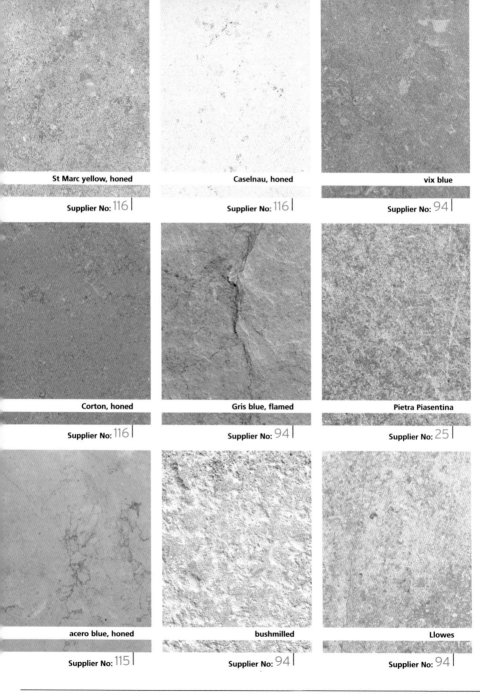

St Marc yellow, honed

Supplier No: 116 |

Caselnau, honed

Supplier No: 116 |

vix blue

Supplier No: 94 |

Corton, honed

Supplier No: 116 |

Gris blue, flamed

Supplier No: 94 |

Pietra Piasentina

Supplier No: 25 |

acero blue, honed

Supplier No: 115 |

bushmilled

Supplier No: 94 |

Llowes

Supplier No: 94 |

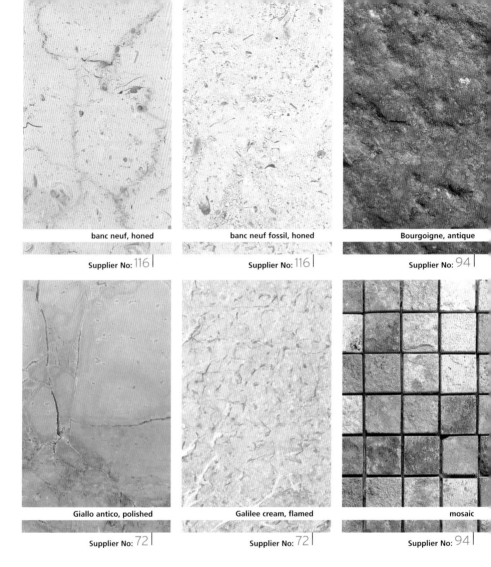

banc neuf, honed
Supplier No: 116

banc neuf fossil, honed
Supplier No: 116

Bourgoigne, antique
Supplier No: 94

Giallo antico, polished
Supplier No: 72

Galilee cream, flamed
Supplier No: 72

mosaic
Supplier No: 94

BUYER INFORMATION
Some types are more easily cut and shaped than others, so check before purchasing. Limestone is suitable both for interior and exterior use. Paler stones are more porous and should be sealed well to avoid staining. Harder stones have coarser grain with inherent nonslip and durable properties and can be used as floor coverings in high-traffic or wet areas.

7.2 Marble & Granite

Smooth, hard, and cool to the touch, both marble and granite provide beautiful patterning that cannot be replicated. Marble is both versatile and easy to work with. Tougher than limestone, it is water-resistant and doesn't show scratches. Highly decorative, like granite it can take a high polish, while impurities form distinctive streaks and clouds to give an illusion of depth and translucency. Once considered a luxury, it is now available at affordable prices.

SPECIFICATIONS

■ **Size:**
Marble: Untreated blocks can be 11½ x 6½ x 5 ft (3.5 x 2 x 1.5m); slabs, tiles, and mosaic vary depending on supplier. Granite: Available in tiles, setts, and slabs of various sizes. Tiles are the cheaper option.

■ **Surface texture:**
Marble: For interiors, highly polished or matte; underfoot, honed.
Granite: Even, grainy, with a visible crystalline structure.

■ **Colors:**
Marble: Veining, streaking, and color variations; pure marble is almost white.
Granite: From gray and green through to yellow and red.

■ **Finish:**
Marble: Smoothing and polishing will give a series of cuts and finishes.
Granite: Depth best appreciated in high-gloss polish, but also flamed, sawn, honed.

■ **Applications:**
Marble: Often used for bathrooms, countertops, wet areas, fireplace surrounds, flooring, interior cladding.
Granite: Used both outside and inside; ideal choice for flooring, countertops, exterior setts, areas of high traffic, cladding.

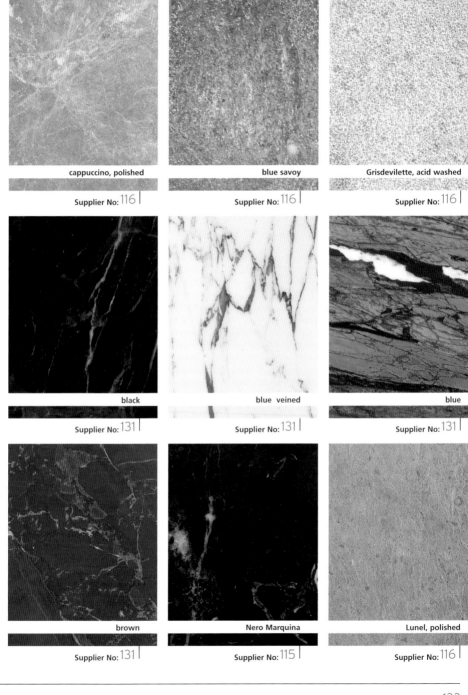

cappuccino, polished

Supplier No: 116 |

blue savoy

Supplier No: 116 |

Grisdevilette, acid washed

Supplier No: 116 |

black

Supplier No: 131 |

blue veined

Supplier No: 131 |

blue

Supplier No: 131 |

brown

Supplier No: 131 |

Nero Marquina

Supplier No: 115 |

Lunel, polished

Supplier No: 116 |

Immensely durable, granite is the toughest of all stones. Available in rich, bold colors, it is usually polished to a hardwearing, high-gloss finish. It is resistant to staining, etching, fading, burning, and air pollution. Some lighter granite needs to be sealed before being polished and/or waxed, but the stone is basically low maintenance.

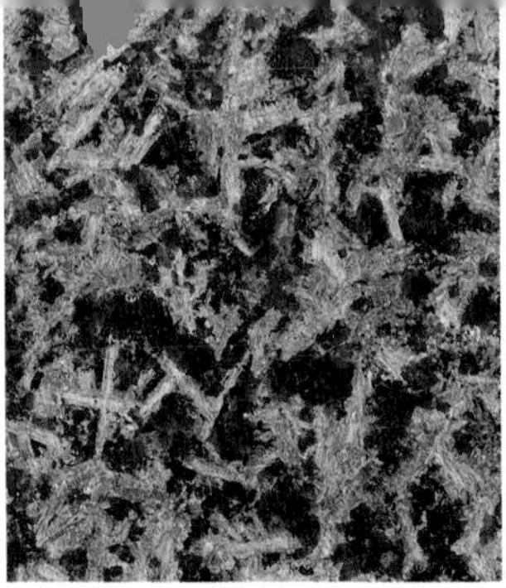

Kinawa bianco, polished

Supplier No: 72

Syenite Monique, polished

Supplier No: 72

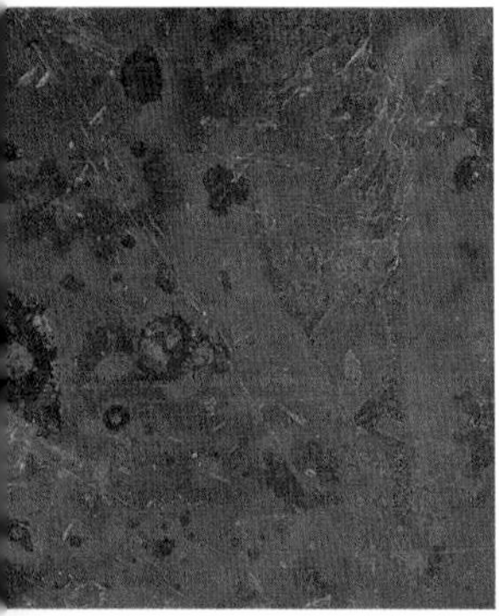

blue

Supplier No: 131

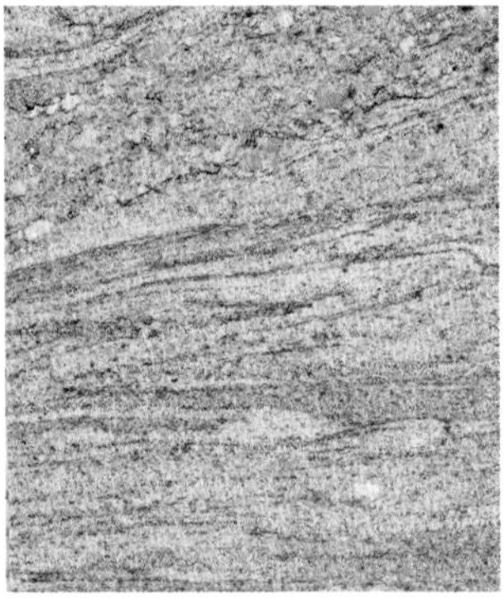

blue & pink

Supplier No: 131

pink

Supplier No: 131

gray

Supplier No: 131

blue

Supplier No: 131

red

Supplier No: 131

Opus Anticato, honed

Supplier No: 72

Bursa beige

Supplier No: 116

Noce, tumbled

Supplier No: 116

Mosaics have always been a popular choice of finish. Available in a wide range of formats (glass, wood, metal, and ceramic). Most mosaics, including stones such as marble, are available as sheets on flexible mesh or paper so are relatively easy to install.

herringbone mosaic

Supplier No: 131

rectangle mosaic

Supplier No: 131

BUYER INFORMATION

Both stones vary enormously in appearance and are available in a variety of finishes (high-gloss and polished are the most popular). Both marble and granite are tougher than limestone so are a good choice for countertops and floors. Both types of stone are popular in bathrooms, but marble will need to be properly sealed whereas granite has an extremely low level of moisture absorption. Granite is extremely hardwearing, but care should be taken with marble.

7.3 Slate

Slate is resilient but less durable than granite. It can be split to expose a unique textured surface with great decorative potential. Cool underfoot and versatile in appearance (from solid shades to speckled patterns), the color and rugged texture of slate displays an appealing lack of uniformity and a range of hues from gray, green and blue, to black.

SPECIFICATIONS

- **Size:**
Available as tiles or slabs, tile sizes vary according to supplier. Maximum slab size is 78 x 39 x 1¼ in. (2000 x 1000 x 32mm).

- **Surface texture:**
Clean and minimalist or rustic—depends on the finish.

- **Colors:**
Blues and greens to silver-gray and black.

- **Finish:**
Honed, flamed, cleft/riven, sanded, polished, varnished to let colors shine through.

- **Applications:**
Floors, cladding, stairs, steps, pavers, shelves.

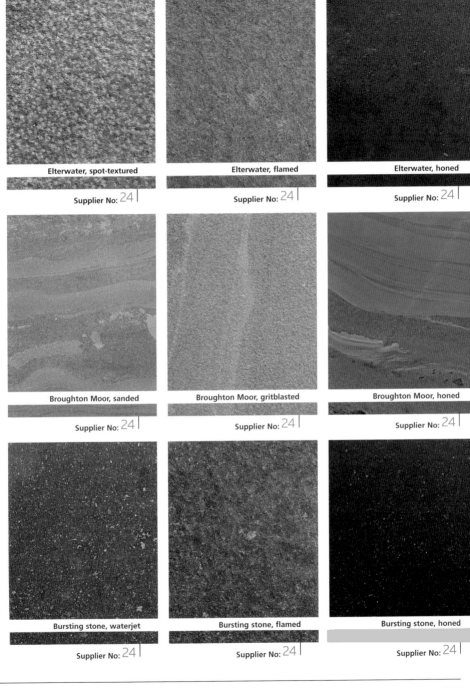

Elterwater, spot-textured

Supplier No: 24

Elterwater, flamed

Supplier No: 24

Elterwater, honed

Supplier No: 24

Broughton Moor, sanded

Supplier No: 24

Broughton Moor, gritblasted

Supplier No: 24

Broughton Moor, honed

Supplier No: 24

Bursting stone, waterjet

Supplier No: 24

Bursting stone, flamed

Supplier No: 24

Bursting stone, honed

Supplier No: 24

Slate 137

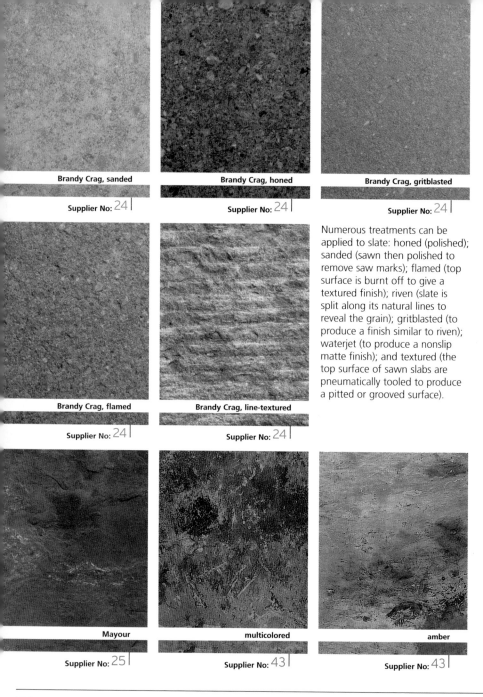

Brandy Crag, sanded

Supplier No: 24

Brandy Crag, honed

Supplier No: 24

Brandy Crag, gritblasted

Supplier No: 24

Numerous treatments can be applied to slate: honed (polished); sanded (sawn then polished to remove saw marks); flamed (top surface is burnt off to give a textured finish); riven (slate is split along its natural lines to reveal the grain); gritblasted (to produce a finish similar to riven); waterjet (to produce a nonslip matte finish); and textured (the top surface of sawn slabs are pneumatically tooled to produce a pitted or grooved surface).

Brandy Crag, flamed

Supplier No: 24

Brandy Crag, line-textured

Supplier No: 24

Mayour

Supplier No: 25

multicolored

Supplier No: 43

amber

Supplier No: 43

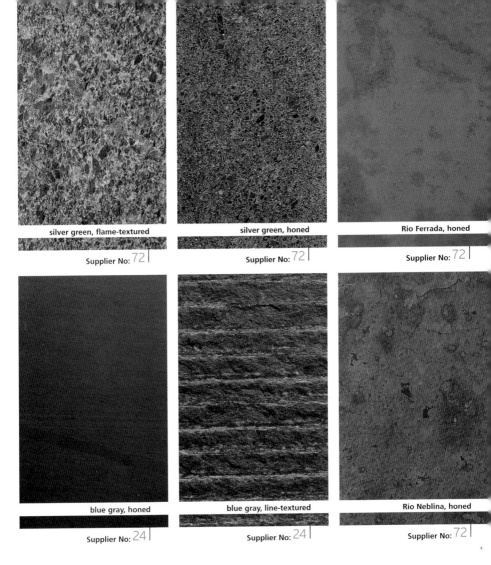

silver green, flame-textured

Supplier No: 72

silver green, honed

Supplier No: 72

Rio Ferrada, honed

Supplier No: 72

blue gray, honed

Supplier No: 24

blue gray, line-textured

Supplier No: 24

Rio Neblina, honed

Supplier No: 72

BUYER INFORMATION

Slate is typically a less expensive option than granite, marble, or limestone, and offers cool, low-maintenance flooring. A penetrating seal is usually required, which will enhance the color of the stone, protect from wear, and ease cleaning and maintenance, but may also change its appearance and increase the slip factor.

For a contemporary look, mix tile sizes in alternating, decorative bands. Complex designs can be achieved by using different finishes of the same stone. Grout can match or contrast stone.

7.4 Natural Options

Sandstone is harder and more durable than limestone; it is resistant to most acids, alkalis, frost, and atmospheric pollution. Color varies between layers and can fade over time. Quartzite with a higher quartz content has a bright texture and color does not fade. Travertine is a popular choice for its beautiful colors and naturally pitted and banded appearance. Basalt is a dark fine-grained volcanic rock, the most common rock type in the earth's crust.

SPECIFICATIONS

■ Size:
Common formats are flags, slabs, setts, and tiles. Standard dimensions will vary depending on stone and supplier.

■ Surface texture:
Sandstone: Rough to medium-grain.
Quartzite: Sugary appearance, medium-grain.
Travertine: Filled or unfilled.
Basalt: Fine-grain.

■ Colors:
Sandstone: Green, gray-blue, gray, brown, dark red/rust, ochre, yellow.
Quartzite: White, gray, reddish.
Travertine: Beige to cream.
Basalt: Dark black, dark gray.

■ Finishes:
Sandstone: Honed, sanded, rough-hewn, polished, flamed, gritblasted, riven.
Quartzite: Natural, cleft, honed.
Travertine: Filled, honed, aged, polished, chipped, brushed.
Basalt: Polished, flamed, honed, sawn.

■ Applications:
Sandstone: Wall cladding, steps, light- to medium-traffic areas.
Quartzite: Flooring (honed), wall cladding.
Travertine: Generally used on flooring, countertops, and walls.
Basalt: Countertops, flooring, walls.

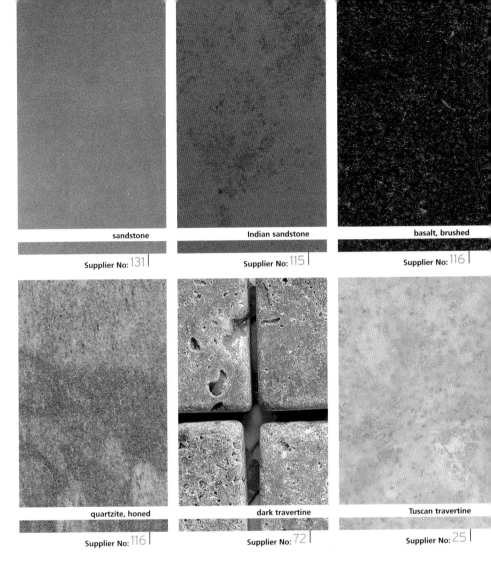

sandstone

Supplier No: 131

Indian sandstone

Supplier No: 115

basalt, brushed

Supplier No: 116

quartzite, honed

Supplier No: 116

dark travertine

Supplier No: 72

Tuscan travertine

Supplier No: 25

BUYER INFORMATION
Natural antiskid qualities make sandstone ideal for floors. It can be sealed, which will protect it from staining, but will leave natural characteristics visible. Quartzite is hardwearing, weather- and heat-resistant but is difficult to shape and cut. Travertine can be used prefilled or unfilled (usually on the exterior of buildings). Basalt is a very hard stone, so it is suitable for internal and external application.

7.5 Irregular

Stone can be precision cut into tiles and slabs, but it is also available in a selection of nonuniform formats. Typically handsorted, the stones are color-matched and glued onto mesh backing. They can be laid down to provide a continuous flow of irregular stones without the rigid joints that tiles demand. Each installation is unique.

SPECIFICATIONS

- **Size:**
Average stone size varies. Mesh-backed formats vary depending upon supplier.

- **Surface texture:**
Depends on type and size of stone.

- **Colors:**
Many to choose from.

- **Finishes:**
Usually irregular, can be bought presealed or unsealed.

- **Applications:**
Floors and walls. Smaller stones are usually used for interior.

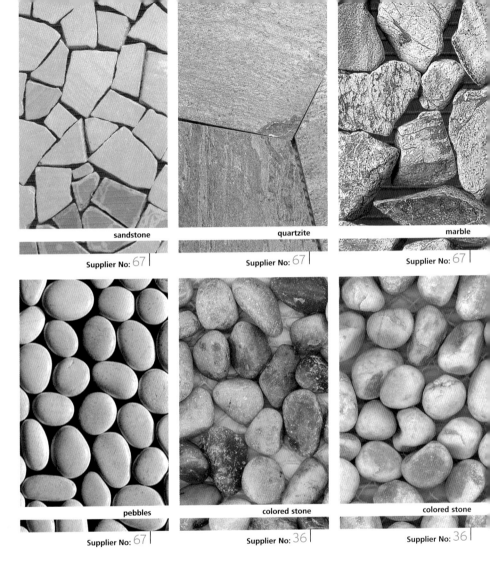

sandstone
Supplier No: 67

quartzite
Supplier No: 67

marble
Supplier No: 67

pebbles
Supplier No: 67

colored stone
Supplier No: 36

colored stone
Supplier No: 36

BUYER INFORMATION

Brightly colored pebbles and natural stones are generally available in a flexible mesh-backed format, which can be grouted, but they can also be found mounted into resin tiles or sheets. Mesh-backed tiles are typically laid on an even, dry substrate, though manufacturers also recommend installing a waterproof membrane before fixing the tiles. Detailed fixing advice is available from suppliers.

8 Clay

Tough and waterproof, tiles are practical, hardwearing, and a great option for walls and floors. A continually evolving area, there is a huge and increasing range available to choose from, and as a relatively inexpensive option, there is plenty of variety to suit any budget.

Aesthetics

Typically laid by hand, clay products like bricks and tiles (ceramic, porcelain, and terracotta) are available in a great number of mass-processed and handmade forms. Brick is better known as a traditional construction material, but the varieties of brick styles and colors available today make it an interesting material for use in contemporary interiors.

Porcelain and ceramic are one of the most popular tile coverings for floors and walls. A relatively inexpensive option, they are available in a wide variety of colors, textures, and formats. Ceramic tiles are the most familiar. Despite the potential for plenty of high-gloss, colorful glazes, this has traditionally been a conservative area with functional white as the mainstay. However, recent years have seen new innovations such as white tiles in larger formats with specialist ceramic textures embossed into the surface. Porcelain gives a more robust finish. Readily available in neutral tones and gently textured surfaces, it has an ability to emulate natural stone while neatly avoiding inherent maintenance issues. Porcelain can also be precision-cut into amazing geometric and irregular-shaped mosaics, some with unusual inserts, such as wood or mother-of-pearl.

As with many other materials, tiles have accrued great benefits from advances in technology: digital printing has had a huge impact on the range of available finishes, for example. Although handpainting and silk screen techniques are still used, digital wizardry extends abstract imagery beyond the boundaries of a single tile, resulting in limitless possibilities of exciting textures and designs. Also available are specialist finishes, such as metallic glazes, and painted effects, such as blackboard tiles. The choice of grout has now moved on from dirt-showing white to colors such as black, red, and blue. Always a popular choice of finish, mosaics are now available in a wide range of formats, materials, colors, and styles. Brightly colored pebbles and natural stones can also be provided in flexible tile format or contained within resin sheets.

Tile collections often come in an assortment of sizes within the same range, automatically providing the option for the creation of pattern. By mixing individual color with plain, or incorporating metallic or glass feature tiles, there is huge potential to experiment with subtle contrasts of textures and tones when creating your own designs.

Additional processed alternatives to ceramic and porcelain include terracotta with its warm tones and pleasing irregularity. With so many individually designed ranges, it can be hard to know where to start choosing, let alone finish. Many tiles have fabulous natural characteristics, coupled with the added advantage of higher performance and lower maintenance than some of their natural counterparts. Cool underfoot, they are also a good choice to combine with underfloor heating.

8.1 Ceramic & Porcelain

Porcelain tiles are resistant to staining and porosity. Available glazed or unglazed, fully vitrified tiles are hardwearing, low maintenance, resistant to chemicals and climate change, and are suitable for use in commercial or domestic heavy-duty flooring and wall finishes. Ceramics are less durable but are still water- and stain-resistant so are suitable for walls and light-duty flooring. Their popularity lies in their versatility: they are available in a variety of clays, glazes, textures, and formats.

SPECIFICATIONS

■ Size:
Many sizes, usually square or rectangular. Edge trims, matching details and borders available.

■ Surface texture:
Ceramic: Handmade tiles provide greater irregularity in texture, color, and thickness.
Porcelain: Varies—polished, flamed for a surface similar to natural stone, or honed to a satin sheen.

■ Colors:
Ceramic: Full spectrum—solid color and decorative motifs.
Porcelain: Natural color shades and subtle surface finishes to suit all budgets.

■ Finish:
Ceramic: Unglazed or glazed, high gloss, matte, and metallic; straight or bevelled edges.

Rectified edges make joints almost invisible.
Porcelain: Plain, rough, or polished.

■ Applications:
Ceramic: Walls and light-duty floors, sills, and splashbacks.
Porcelain: Internal use, floors, walls, splashbacks; can be used outside if fully vitrified.

matte finish

Supplier No: 117

rectangular mosaic

Supplier No: 119

stone effect

Supplier No: 25

matte finish

Supplier No: 117

matte finish

Supplier No: 117

stone effect

Supplier No: 25

broken line

Supplier No: 119

non-uniform square texture

Supplier No: 129

stone effect

Supplier No: 25

wave texture

Supplier No: 36

porcelain stoneware

Supplier No: 36

porcelain stoneware

Supplier No: 36

porcelain stoneware

Supplier No: 36

porcelain stoneware

Supplier No: 36

striped

Supplier No: 117

line texture

Supplier No: 119

composite finish

Supplier No: 117

rectangular ceramic mosaic

Supplier No: 119

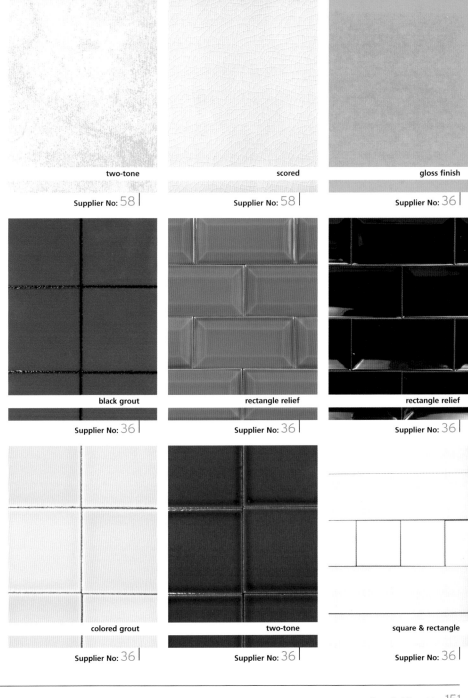

two-tone

Supplier No: 58 |

scored

Supplier No: 58 |

gloss finish

Supplier No: 36 |

black grout

Supplier No: 36 |

rectangle relief

Supplier No: 36 |

rectangle relief

Supplier No: 36 |

colored grout

Supplier No: 36 |

two-tone

Supplier No: 36 |

square & rectangle

Supplier No: 36 |

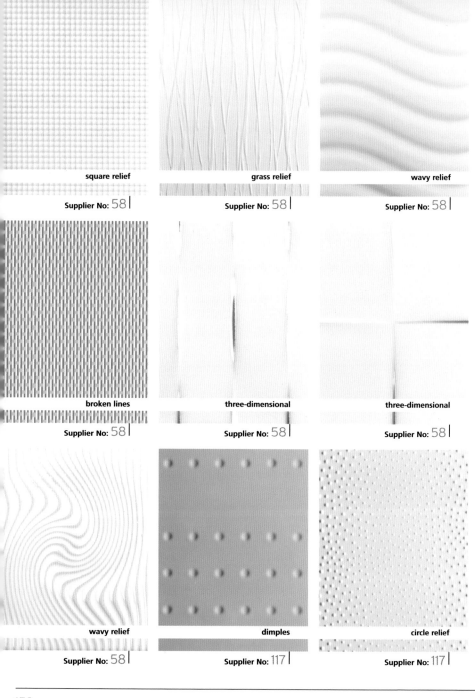

square relief
Supplier No: 58

grass relief
Supplier No: 58

wavy relief
Supplier No: 58

broken lines
Supplier No: 58

three-dimensional
Supplier No: 58

three-dimensional
Supplier No: 58

wavy relief
Supplier No: 58

dimples
Supplier No: 117

circle relief
Supplier No: 117

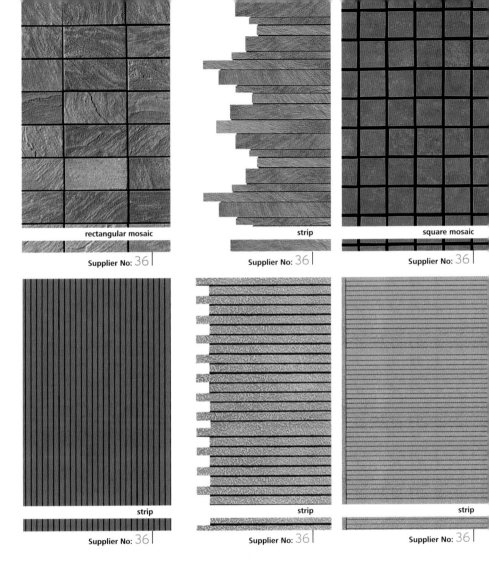

rectangular mosaic

Supplier No: 36 |

strip

Supplier No: 36 |

square mosaic

Supplier No: 36 |

strip

Supplier No: 36 |

strip

Supplier No: 36 |

strip

Supplier No: 36 |

BUYER INFORMATION
Ceramics are available in edge trims, matching details, and borders, but the edges can look less crisp than porcelain. They are easy to keep clean, but can be cold and slippery underfoot, and are less likely to withstand knocks from heavy objects. Color may also vary between batches. Porcelain offers a practical and relatively cheap alternative to stone. Available in a variety of textures, from stone-like forms to smooth solid color, it also comes as incised tiles, precision-cut to provide a similar effect to mosaic but with an immaculate uniformity. In general, ceramic tiles are easier to bond and usually easier to cut than porcelain tiles.

8.2 Specialist

What was once seen as specialist is now fairly standard. Choice has increased so much that the options are almost endless—examples include hand-painted or digitally printed tiles; tiles fired with metallic glaze to simulate silver, bronze, or pewter in polished or satin finishes; and tiled inserts including inlays of frosted glass and metal. More traditional formats include classic pottery style, elongated tiles, and reproduction tiles.

SPECIFICATIONS

■ **Size:**
Many different sizes and shapes available.

■ **Surface texture:**
Ceramic and porcelain, stone, glass, metal; machine- and handcut; special order with mother-of-pearl, wood inserts.

■ **Colors:**
Full spectrum.

■ **Finish:**
Unglazed or glazed, textured, bush-hammered, matte, metallic, polished, satin, honed.

■ **Applications:**
Walls and light-duty floors, sills, splashbacks.

■ **Options:**
Mosaics with flexible mesh or paper backing.

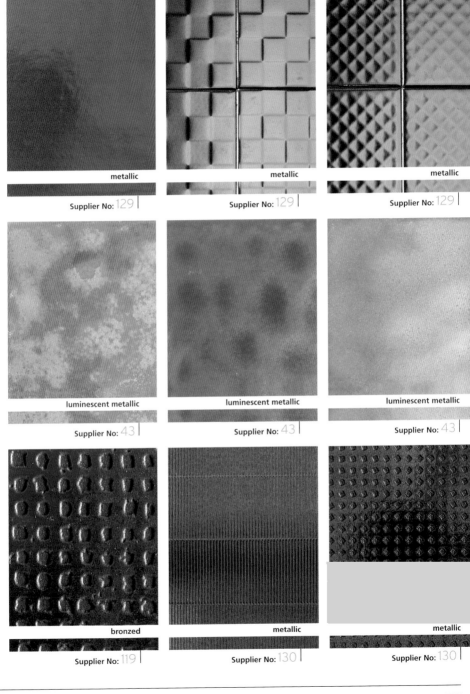

metallic

Supplier No: 129

metallic

Supplier No: 129

metallic

Supplier No: 129

luminescent metallic

Supplier No: 43

luminescent metallic

Supplier No: 43

luminescent metallic

Supplier No: 43

bronzed

Supplier No: 119

metallic

Supplier No: 130

metallic

Supplier No: 130

handpainted

Supplier No: 131

screenprinted

Supplier No: 131

handpainted

Supplier No: 131

handpainted, irregular size

Supplier No: 131

handpainted

Supplier No: 43

handpainted

Supplier No: 43

handpainted

Supplier No: 43

metal insert

Supplier No: 131

porcelain & glass composite

Supplier No: 129

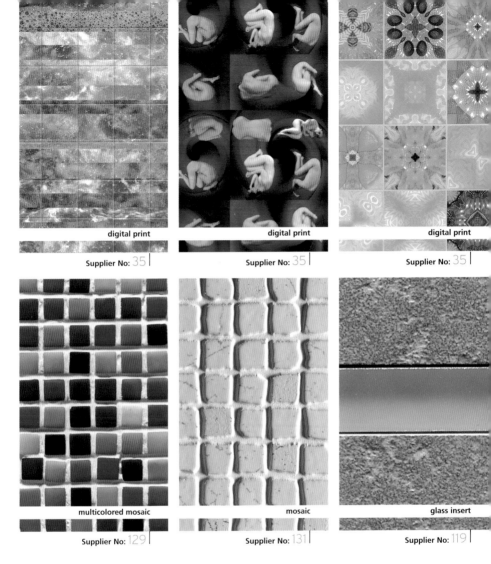

digital print

Supplier No: 35

digital print

Supplier No: 35

digital print

Supplier No: 35

multicolored mosaic

Supplier No: 129

mosaic

Supplier No: 131

glass insert

Supplier No: 119

BUYER INFORMATION

Digital technology means you can create your own design, transferring an image of your choice onto a single ceramic tile, or a across whole wall, if desired.

Ceramic and porcelain mosaics can be provided as sheets on flexible mesh or paper so are relatively easy to install. Some ranges include feature tiles of materials, such as handcut mother-of-pearl, metals, or wood. Metallic mosaics and textured metallic reliefs are available at a fraction of the cost of sheet metal and are often better suited to the application.

8.3 Terracotta

Made from clay, formats include handmade, manufactured, antique, and new. Handmade tiles provide greater irregularity in texture, color, and thickness. Antique terracotta (fired in wood-burning kilns) gives varied color and a less uniform texture than those fired in gas- or coal-fired kilns. Terracotta is available in a variety of shades, reflecting the native color of their origin. Blended clays may produce a mix of colors across the floor.

SPECIFICATIONS

Size:
Available in a variety of sizes and shapes, but machine-cut tiles are traditionally square.

Surface texture:
Handmade tiles are irregular in texture, color, and thickness; machine-made tiles are more uniform, but can be aged.

Colors:
Pale pink, ochre, dark red.

Finishes:
Unglazed or glazed; glazed terracotta is available in gloss, satin, matte, and even metallic.

Applications:
Almost exclusively used as a traditional flooring.

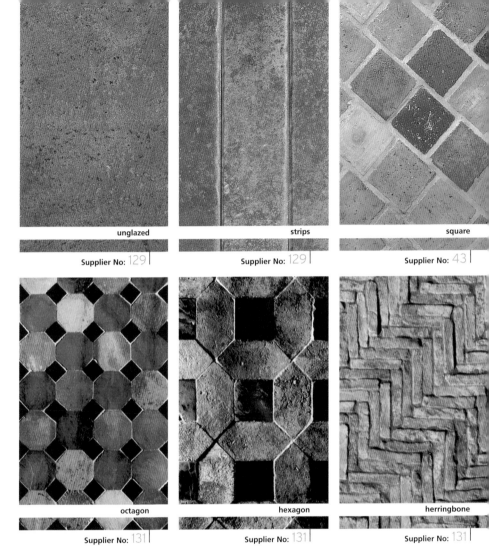

unglazed

Supplier No: 129

strips

Supplier No: 129

square

Supplier No: 43

octagon

Supplier No: 131

hexagon

Supplier No: 131

herringbone

Supplier No: 131

BUYER INFORMATION

Terracotta is often sold by stone dealers and is cheaper than limestone or granite, although reclaimed tiles can be relatively expensive. Glazed terracotta is now available in a variety of colors, textures, patterns, and styles. Tiles are highly porous, so require maintenance, but the rustic look improves with age. Even cheaper than terracotta, quarry tiles are made from unrefined high-silica clays, which are a uniform texture and color but do not gain patina with age. Terracotta is cool underfoot but absorbs heat, so it is a good choice for underfloor heating. For exterior use, rain-screen cladding systems are now available in durable, large-format masonry block.

8.4 Bricks & Pavers

Handmade until the mid-nineteenth century, with irregularities and wide variations in color and texture, bricks today are a more uniform product. This doesn't, however, preclude their use in interior design—they can be left exposed as a final wall finish, offering a textural backdrop that lends itself to pattern and unpretentious warmth.

SPECIFICATIONS

■ **Size:**
A wide variety of common sizes available, but roughly:
US standard: 4 x 8 x 2¼ in.
UK standard: 102 x 215 x 65mm.

■ **Surface texture:**
Rough, pitted, smooth, glazed.

■ **Colors:**
Different clays produce different natural colors.

■ **Finishes:**
Many grades of finish.
Glazed, unglazed, varnished, sandcoated.

■ **Applications:**
Walkways, walls.

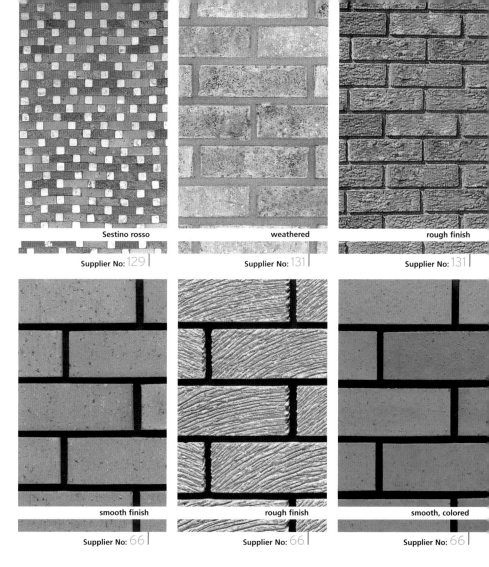

Sestino rosso

Supplier No: 129

weathered

Supplier No: 131

rough finish

Supplier No: 131

smooth finish

Supplier No: 66

rough finish

Supplier No: 66

smooth, colored

Supplier No: 66

BUYER INFORMATION
Available in a wide variety of shapes and tones, bricks are an extremely versatile material. Not just for textured walls, they are warmer underfoot than stone or ceramics. Manufactured in a number of grades, engineering bricks are the most durable—they are resistant to impact, wear, frost, and chemicals.
Handmade bricks can be expensive; locally manufactured bricks are the cheapest option.
Salvaged bricks can be found at specialist suppliers, but can be more expensive than new ones.

9 Glass

The glass industry is constantly developing, and now responds to the demands of safety, security, and thermal insulation while remaining decorative and practical. Thanks to its versatility, a huge range of innovative glasses, finishes, and colors are now used in domestic applications.

Aesthetics

Technology has ensured that developments in this field have responded to increased demands on structural and technical specifications and glass can be produced economically, in large formats of varying thicknesses. With so many products on the market, this chapter cannot hope to cover the technical specifications, specialist coatings, or interactive possibilities of external glazing, but concentrates instead on smaller-scale fittings and fixtures for interior applications. Interior glass now offers more than clean lines and high-performance transparency. Up-to-the-minute machinery and fully automated processes provide a huge range of textures, glowing colors, and precision finishes over extensive glazed surfaces. While some products are only available through large-order commercial contracts, independent specialist glass manufacturers are reacting to domestic demands to offer ranges of standard patterns, as well as tailormade bespoke designs, including letters and logos, plus handmade tiles and architectural wall panels saturated with color.

Surprisingly durable, there are many innovative interior applications with interesting decorative effects that manipulate texture, color, and opacity. Windows, doors, partitions, floors, stairtreads, balustrades, shower screens, splashbacks, furniture, mirrors, and countertops now are all available in glass. Finishes include the subtle contrasts and intricate designs of acid-etching and sandblasting, decorative laminated wall panels, shiny embossed patterns, vibrant enameled color, subtle body tints, distinctive mirrors, unique and eye-catching screen-printed designs, and innovative glass blocks. On a smaller scale, glass mosaics are now available with varying degrees of transparency, color saturation, finishes, and coatings. If it's large areas of color you are after, then consider colored enameled glass; sheets of glass painted with an opaque color or a transparent tint to great effect. Kilnformed glass can look spectacular if silicone-mounted onto toughened glass and backlit, and is available in a choice of standard patterns, or bespoke designs, as well as finishes.

In addition to commercial manufacturers, smaller design companies are now focusing on recycled products, resulting in unusual glasses created from low-value waste such as televisions and car windows. Specialist "craft" glasses can be used for feature windows or walls, creating a kind of contemporary stained glass in multicolored artworks. Careful consideration of lighting possibilities is an essential part of the success of any installation, taking advantage of the unique iridescent surface of decorative glass—etched and sandblasted glass will gently diffuse light according to the pattern; laminated glass with a colored inner layer will glow; opaque floors look fabulous when underlit.

Whether transparent, translucent, or opaque, there are limitless durable and decorative finishes and an abundance of manufacturing techniques to choose from for an assortment of spaces. Glass treatments can manipulate transparency, color, and pattern to great effect and glass itself is functional and flexible, capable of resolving many complex design requirements. However, although it may be a versatile material not all applications are appropriate for hasty DIY fabrication. For example, glass partitions can provide separation, transparency, and a degree of privacy, but may scratch or break if hit by a hard object and so need to be toughened or laminated for domestic use.

9.1 Translucent

Acid-etching and sandblasting offer transparency and translucency while allowing light transmission and privacy. The former gives a smooth, soft, uniform surface, with a number of tones and levels. Sandblasting is more tactile, and can be used to produce a deeply carved, opaque finish. The two techniques can be used individually or in combination. Toughened, safety, and wired glass, meanwhile, offer increased strength and exceptional durability.

SPECIFICATIONS

■ **Size:**
Standard-float glass: Average sheet size ⅟₁₆–1 in. (2–25mm) thick, 126 in. (3210mm) wide.

Textured glass: Typically ⅛–¼ in. (4–6mm thick), 52 x 84 in. (1320 x 2140mm) average sheet size.

Laminated glass: Typically three-ply, from ⅛–1¾ in. (4.4–45mm) thick, 126 x 78⅜ in. (3200 x 2000mm) average sheet size.

■ **Surface texture:**
Complex patterns achieved by combining techniques that control transparency.

■ **Finishes:**
Bespoke designs (sandblasted; acid-etched); one or both faces can be treated.

■ **Options:**
Toughened, laminated, colored, backlit, underlit.

■ **Applications:**
Floor panels, partitions, screens, splashbacks, doors, windows, stairtreads, lighting, tabletops, shelves, balustrades, signage.

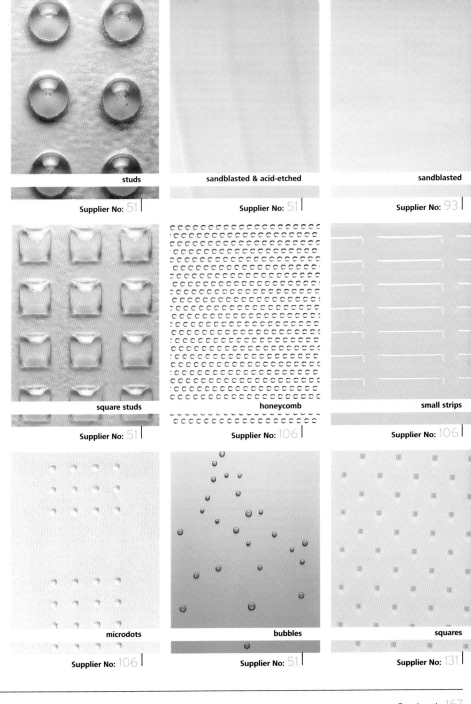

studs

Supplier No: 51

sandblasted & acid-etched

Supplier No: 51

sandblasted

Supplier No: 93

square studs

Supplier No: 51

honeycomb

Supplier No: 106

small strips

Supplier No: 106

microdots

Supplier No: 106

bubbles

Supplier No: 51

squares

Supplier No: 131

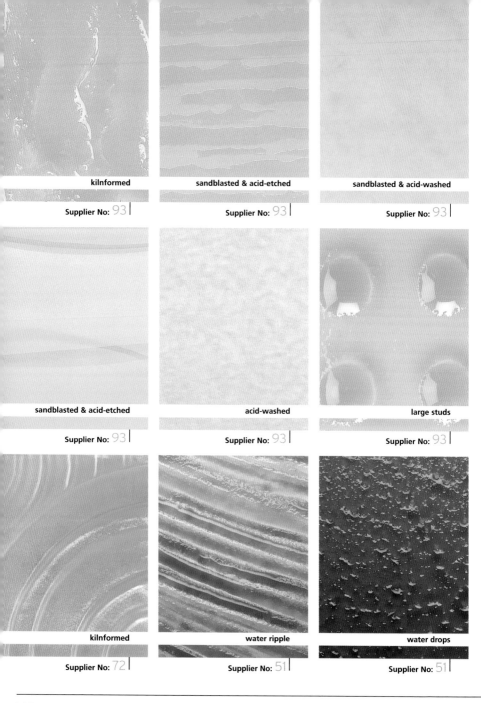

kilnformed

Supplier No: 93

sandblasted & acid-etched

Supplier No: 93

sandblasted & acid-washed

Supplier No: 93

sandblasted & acid-etched

Supplier No: 93

acid-washed

Supplier No: 93

large studs

Supplier No: 93

kilnformed

Supplier No: 72

water ripple

Supplier No: 51

water drops

Supplier No: 51

Materials such as fabric, wood, and metal can be sandwiched between two layers of glass to form laminated panels. They provide unique visual effects and are ideal for constructing feature walls or partitions without compromising views or finish. Color can also be added with a resin interlayer to achieve a high-gloss finish, translucent or opaque, to both sides. Laminated panels are extremely effective, but become difficult to handle if large.

laminated fine cloth

Supplier No: 51

laminated leaf

Supplier No: 51

laminated cloth

Supplier No: 51

laminated color

Supplier No: 51

laminated mesh

Supplier No: 51

BUYER INFORMATION
Sandblasting provides a less slippery finish for stairtreads. Kilnformed glass is suitable for privacy screens, doors, and feature pieces, internally and externally. Acid-etching offers a hardwearing alternative to cheaper vinyl applications. Glass can be fully processed, and is available in toughened and laminated form.
Laminated panels are ideal for constructing subtle feature walls or internal partitions without compromising views or finish, they are the perfect solution when glass is viewable from both sides.

9.2 Blocks

Often dismissed as overpatterned with "craft" effects, technological developments in this field have produced a number of new forms and finishes worthy of any home. Contemporary designs combine the best of structural possibilities with translucency and can provide effective screening to dramatic effect.

SPECIFICATIONS

■ **Size:**
Wide array of block shapes and sizes.Square blocks are typically 8 x 8 x 3⅛ in. (190 x 190 x 80mm).

■ **Surface texture:**
Variety of patterns, from clear to opaque.

■ **Finishes:**
Clear, frosted, reeded, rippled, tinted, mirrored.

■ **Options:**
Clear, opaque, colored, patterned, backlit, underlit.

■ **Applications:**
Partitions, walls, screens, window openings, flooring.

bubbles

Supplier No: 53 |

bark texture

Supplier No: 88 |

square texture

Supplier No: 88 |

opalescent

Supplier No: 88 |

solar reflective

Supplier No: 88 |

misty triangle

Supplier No: 88 |

BUYER INFORMATION

Blocks are now available in a number of shapes beyond the original square (e.g. circular, rectangular, and triangular) and a range of colors. In addition to gently diffusing light, they possess inherent sound- and heat-insulating properties.

For installation, specialist mortars or a frame system may be required. For floors, precast panels are available, and a well-prepared substrate is essential.

9.3 Decorative

Used for centuries for decorative and intricate walls and floors, glass mosaics are now obtainable in easy-to-handle sheets. With varying degrees of transparency, color, and texture, glass mosaics offer a welcome smaller-scale finish. If it's large blocks of color you are after, then consider colored enameled glass; sheets of glass painted with an opaque color or a transparent tint can create a great effect.

SPECIFICATIONS

■ Size:
Mosaic: A variety of tile and sheet sizes, but typically ¾ x ¾ x ⅛ in. (20 x 20 x 4mm) tiles and 12 x 12 in. (300 x 300mm) sheets.
Screen prints: Maximum printed area 71 x 142 in. (1800 x 3600mm)
Mirror: 126 x 236 in. (3210 x 6000mm) maximum.

Laminated glass: Typically three-ply, from ⅛–1¾ in. (4.4–45mm) thick, 126 x 78⅜ in. (3200 x 2000mm) maximum sheet size.

■ Surface texture:
Mosaic: Variety of patterns; square, circular, rectangular, and aligned or staggered joints.

■ Finishes:
Pearlescent, mirror, matte, shiny, silvered, screen-printed.

■ Options:
Aligned/staggered joints.

■ Applications:
Light-duty flooring, walls, screens, splashbacks.

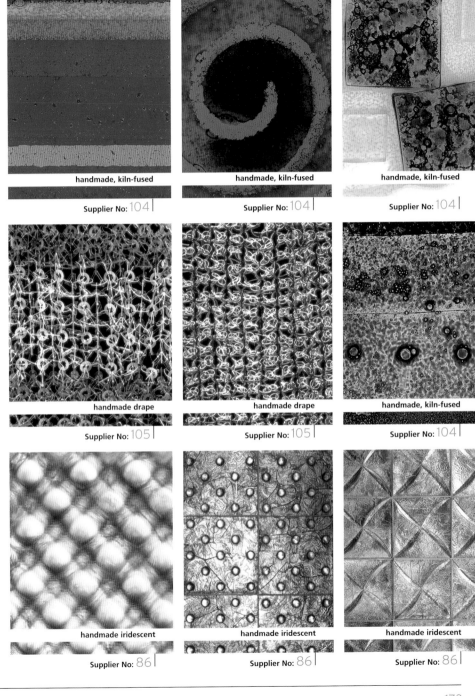

handmade, kiln-fused

handmade, kiln-fused

handmade, kiln-fused

handmade drape

handmade drape

handmade, kiln-fused

handmade iridescent

handmade iridescent

handmade iridescent

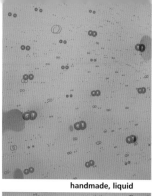

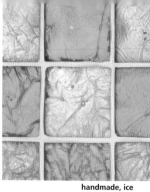

handmade, liquid

handmade, liquid

handmade, ice

Supplier No: 86

Supplier No: 86

Supplier No: 86

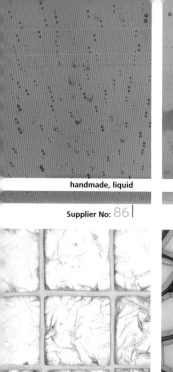

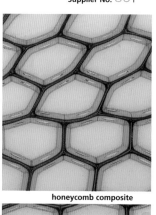

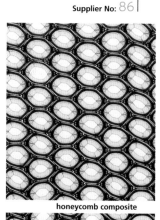

handmade, ice

honeycomb composite

honeycomb composite

Supplier No: 86

Supplier No: 26

Supplier No: 26

sandblast mosaic

sandblast mosaic

sandblast studs

Supplier No: 72

Supplier No: 72

Supplier No: 72

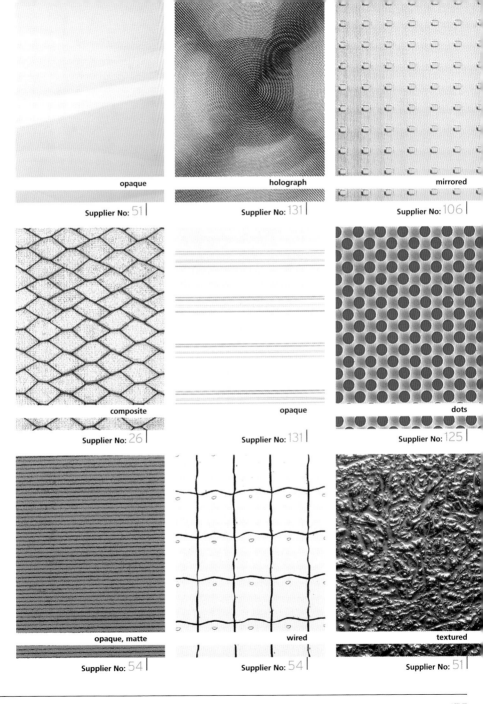

opaque

Supplier No: 51

holograph

Supplier No: 131

mirrored

Supplier No: 106

composite

Supplier No: 26

opaque

Supplier No: 131

dots

Supplier No: 125

opaque, matte

Supplier No: 54

wired

Supplier No: 54

textured

Supplier No: 51

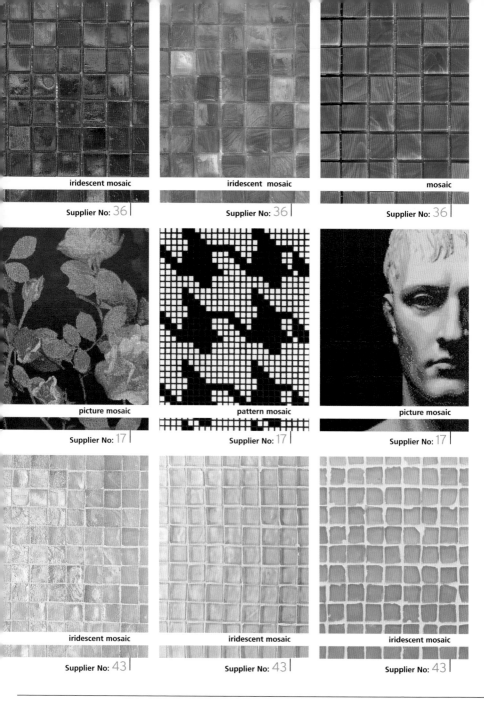

iridescent mosaic

Supplier No: 36

iridescent mosaic

Supplier No: 36

mosaic

Supplier No: 36

picture mosaic

Supplier No: 17

pattern mosaic

Supplier No: 17

picture mosaic

Supplier No: 17

iridescent mosaic

Supplier No: 43

iridescent mosaic

Supplier No: 43

iridescent mosaic

Supplier No: 43

Although still in the development stages, there is great decorative potential for recycled glass. Molded and kilnformed into tiles and slabs, these handmade products vary, to great effect, according to raw material.

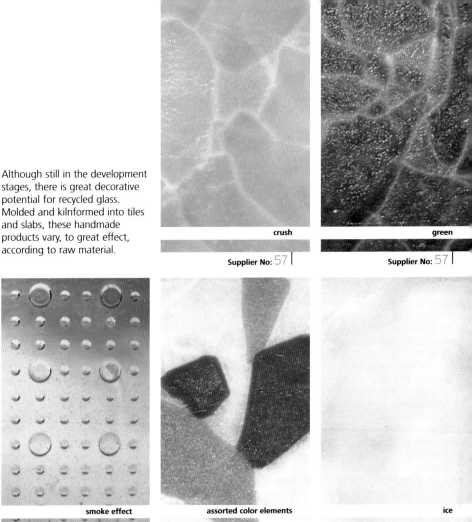

crush

Supplier No: 57

green

Supplier No: 57

smoke effect

Supplier No: 57

assorted color elements

Supplier No: 57

ice

Supplier No: 57

BUYER INFORMATION
Colored enameled and tinted glass offer color stability and are excellent for glossy feature walls. There are a number of specialist suppliers who can provide exquisite handmade tiles and architectural wall panels saturated with color. They often produce ranges of standard patterns as well as tailormade, bespoke designs. However, such applications can be high maintenance to keep clean.

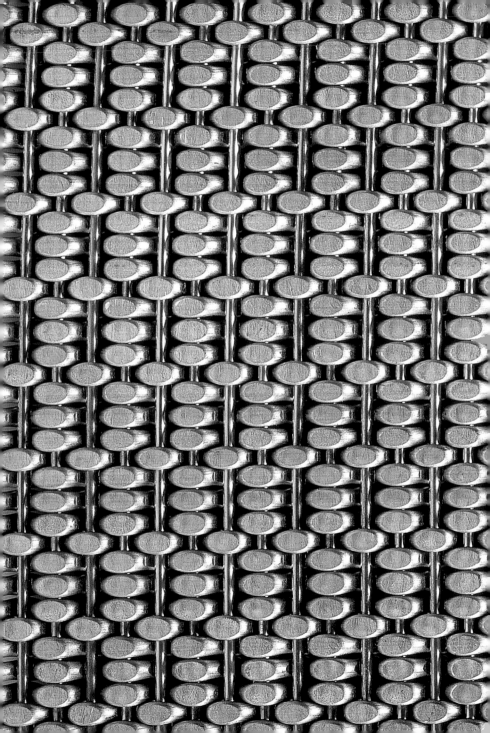

10

Metal

Metal is already used widely for the smaller details of domestic interiors. The larger, more commercial formats were originally deemed suitable only for industrial settings. However, over the last decade, assisted by developments in manufacturing techniques that now allow mass production, many metals have been increasingly commandeered for a domestic context.

Aesthetics

Metal is most familiar for its functional use as a structural element, providing a supporting framework for floors, walls, and windows. But there are plenty of metals used now as functional and decorative finishes for wall panels, floors, stairs, splashbacks, and countertops. Utilitarian in appearance, the clean lines and defined edges of metals provides sharp and stark contrast to nonuniform elements, such as stone or wood, or the softness of textiles and carpet.

Manufacturing techniques have allowed many types of metal to be mass-produced in rigid sheets at thinner gauges. With extensive methods of manufacture (metal can be welded, bolted, soldered, and seamed), the possibilities are endless. Most familiar are sheet metals, such as stainless steel and aluminum. When stainless steel first came to the forefront in the late 1980s, it was held in high regard as the ultimate in urban chic. These days, wall-to-wall stainless steel looks rather dated, but if applied with a little restraint, it can retain an understated appeal. Stainless steel and aluminum are widely available in prefabricated ranges of precision-cut and processed decorative effects: high-gloss coatings, embossed relief patterns, perforated sheets, and are even woven or crimped into light-diffusing meshes and screens. With an assortment of finishes to consider (including polished, matte, and brushed), there is plenty of opportunity to provide texture and contrast.

Sheet metal offers the advantage of providing extensive lengths of seamless surfaces, and is a popular choice for countertops, but the compromise between form and function should always be considered. Although stainless steel can provide a single uniform finish, it will also reveal every grease mark, and while easy to clean, it cannot be considered low maintenance. Aluminum offers a less durable, less shiny finish, but without the same level of maintenance.

In terms of look, other metals to consider for interior surfaces are copper, which gives warm tones and can be polished, smooth, or relief, but tarnishes easily. Zinc is one of the softest metals: it dulls and marks over time, developing an appealing natural worn look. Salvaged metals are also popular. Commercial kitchen units or industrial shelving may be time-consuming to restore but have a ready-made timeworn patina.

No longer treated as background detail, metal is now much more user-friendly and can be used for a number of interior applications; perforated, dividing wall panels; gridded panels for stairs and walkways; seamless countertops; and textured wall finishes. Manufacturers provide off-the-shelf products and bespoke finishes. Too much metal may look rather "high-tech" but get the balance right and your interior will be both striking and functional.

10.1 Sheet

Increasingly popular in the home, metals are used for a range of interior applications. Stainless steel, available in a range of finishes, coatings, and colors is the most commonly used. Advances in technology have allowed intricate finishes with textured, embossed, and acid-etched patterns. Although decorative, such surfaces are also practical, hiding dents and scratches. Sheet metal can be highly polished to provide a mirror surface that, unlike glass, won't shatter.

SPECIFICATIONS

■ **Size:**
Sheet and tile sizes vary depending upon manufacturer.

■ **Surface texture:**
Plain, patterned, embossed, acid-etched.

■ **Finishes:**
Depends on grade of metal. Stainless steel: Mirror polished, brushed, beadblasted, satin. Aluminum: Mill finish, satin and brush polishes, anodized, plastic coated, painted.

■ **Applications:**
Flooring, stairways, cladding, worktops, transitional areas, panels, doors.

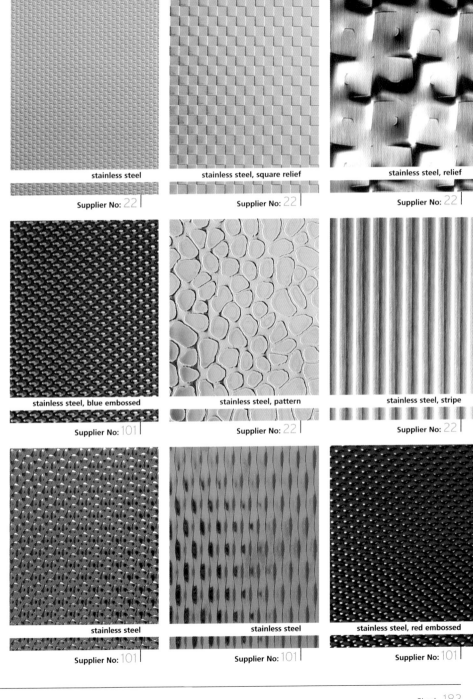

stainless steel

Supplier No: 22

stainless steel, square relief

Supplier No: 22

stainless steel, relief

Supplier No: 22

stainless steel, blue embossed

Supplier No: 101

stainless steel, pattern

Supplier No: 22

stainless steel, stripe

Supplier No: 22

stainless steel

Supplier No: 101

stainless steel

Supplier No: 101

stainless steel, red embossed

Supplier No: 101

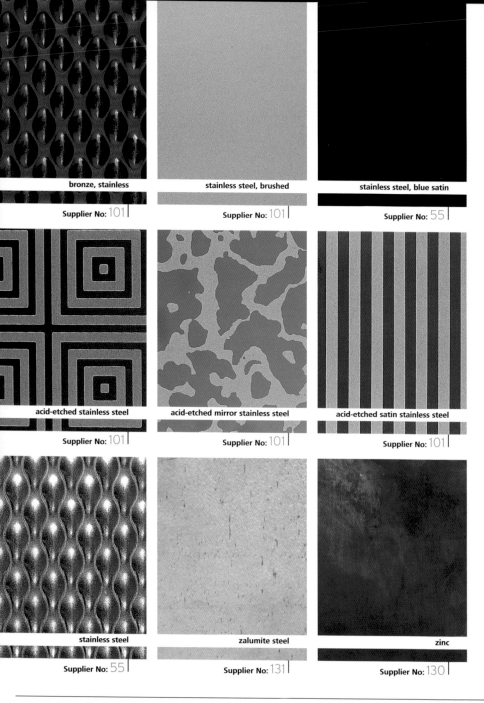

bronze, stainless

Supplier No: 101

stainless steel, brushed

Supplier No: 101

stainless steel, blue satin

Supplier No: 55

acid-etched stainless steel

Supplier No: 101

acid-etched mirror stainless steel

Supplier No: 101

acid-etched satin stainless steel

Supplier No: 101

stainless steel

Supplier No: 55

zalumite steel

Supplier No: 131

zinc

Supplier No: 130

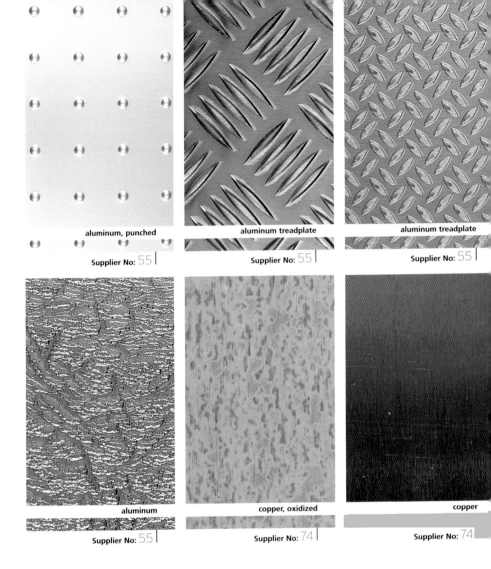

aluminum, punched
Supplier No: 55

aluminum treadplate
Supplier No: 55

aluminum treadplate
Supplier No: 55

aluminum
Supplier No: 55

copper, oxidized
Supplier No: 74

copper
Supplier No: 74

BUYER INFORMATION

Stainless steel work surfaces are hygienic, heatproof, durable, and can be welded together into seamless units. However, they require high maintenance as they scratch easily and show watermarks. Alternatives, such as zinc, are more pliable, easily molded into countertops, and zinc acquires an interesting patina over time. Aluminum is durable, lightweight, and relatively cheap. Easier to maintain than stainless steel, aluminum won't show every finger mark or scratch. Highly resistant to corrosion, aluminum won't shatter and it provides a less clinical aesthetic than stainless steel. Floor tiles may provide contrast in texture but can be noisy and cold underfoot.

10.2 Perforated

Useful for both interior and exterior applications, perforated panels offer a lightweight and versatile solution to varying degrees of transparency, as well as providing natural ventilation and permitting light diffusion. They should be used sparingly to avoid a highly industrial aesthetic.

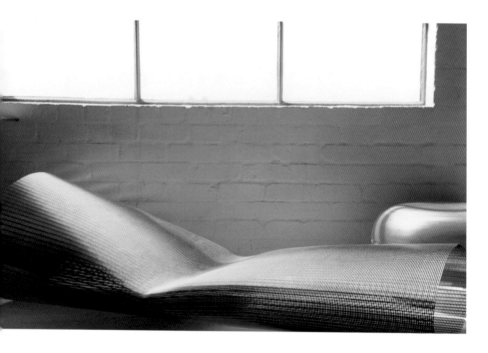

SPECIFICATIONS

■ **Size:**
Sheets vary depending on manufacturer.

■ **Surface texture:**
Different effects can be achieved, depending upon diameter and frequency of holes.

■ **Finishes:**
Satin and brush polishes, painted.

■ **Applications:**
Furniture, balustrades, paneling, solar protection, ventilation panels, wall cladding.

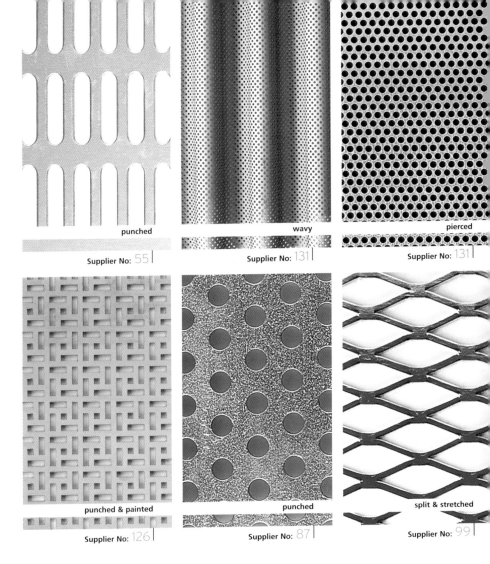

punched

Supplier No: 55

wavy

Supplier No: 131

pierced

Supplier No: 131

punched & painted

Supplier No: 126

punched

Supplier No: 87

split & stretched

Supplier No: 99

BUYER INFORMATION

Perforated plates and decorative grills are available in a multitude of specifications and metals: aluminum, brass, copper, mild steel, galvanized steel, stainless steel, and special alloys. State-of-the-art computer-controlled presses provide high accuracy and a number of different patterns: round, square, oblong, straight-lined, and staggered. Galvanized steel looks more industrial but is cheaper.

10.3 Wire & Weave

Predominantly for commercial use, there is a huge variety of wire products and specialist meshes available: woven wire cloths, wire mesh screens, crimped and cable woven wire meshes, welded metal meshes, and stainless steel cable net. Simple and effective, weaves are versatile and strong, and often self-supporting.

SPECIFICATIONS

■ **Size:**
Available in panels or rolls,
sizes vary depending on manufacturer.

■ **Surface texture:**
All normal grades of stainless steel, electro-polished after manufacture.

■ **Finishes:**
Contrasting surface textures depending on density, texture, transparency of mesh.

■ **Applications:**
Balustrades, suspended ceilings, room dividers, wall coverings, shelves, decking.

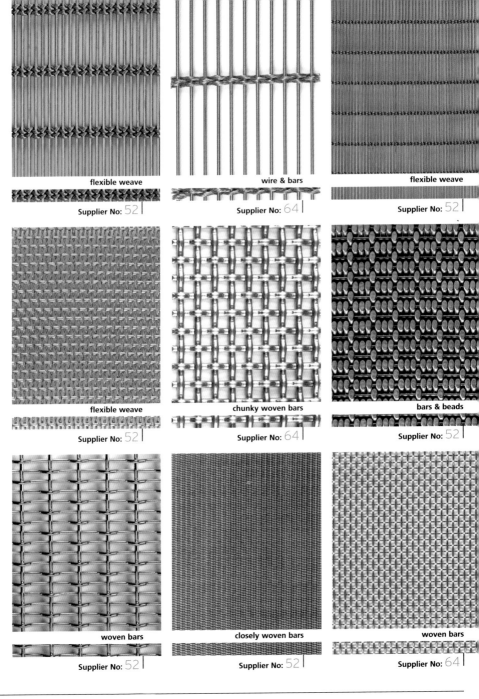

flexible weave

Supplier No: 52

wire & bars

Supplier No: 64

flexible weave

Supplier No: 52

flexible weave

Supplier No: 52

chunky woven bars

Supplier No: 64

bars & beads

Supplier No: 52

woven bars

Supplier No: 52

closely woven bars

Supplier No: 52

woven bars

Supplier No: 64

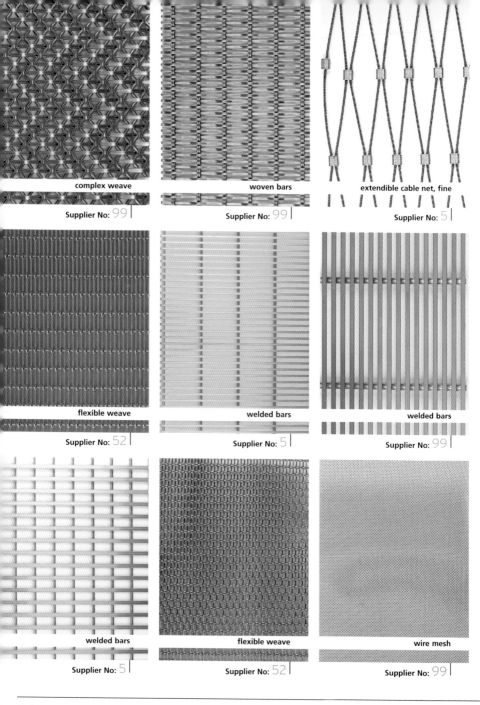

complex weave

Supplier No: 99

woven bars

Supplier No: 99

extendible cable net, fine

Supplier No: 5

flexible weave

Supplier No: 52

welded bars

Supplier No: 5

welded bars

Supplier No: 99

welded bars

Supplier No: 5

flexible weave

Supplier No: 52

wire mesh

Supplier No: 99

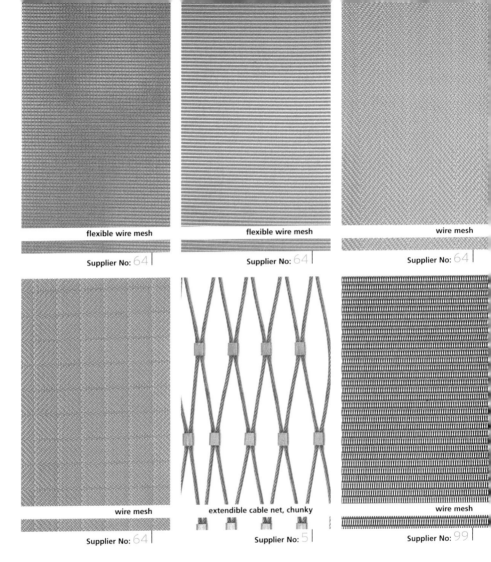

flexible wire mesh

flexible wire mesh

wire mesh

wire mesh

extendible cable net, chunky

wire mesh

BUYER INFORMATION

Woven wire allows for an infinite amount of applications, transparencies and optical effects (depending on which face of mesh is displayed), from 6 in. (152mm) aperture to fine weaves. Lighter meshes are generally available in rolls, while heavier welded products are manufactured in panels. Nonstandard meshes are usually available to order.

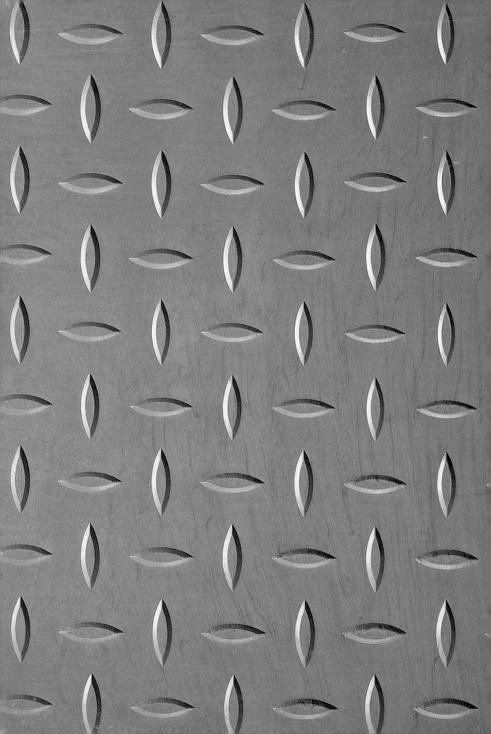

11 Durables

This section covers a multitude of finishes, including rubber, linoleum, vinyl, and acrylic. Suffering from something of an image problem, some of these materials have experienced years of neglect. However, new techniques producing vivid colors and plenty of eye-catching textures, patterns, and finishes have seen an increase in their popularity.

Aesthetics

Most manufactured materials display some natural characteristics, but the addition of silicas, acrylic resin, and pigments transforms them beyond their original state. Preformed off-site into sheets, tiles, or slabs, they are designed to suit specific demands. These materials offer significant practical advantages, being low maintenance and high performance; they are available in a wide variety of textures, finishes, and colors.

Recent years have seen a revival of sheet flooring. Previously considered relatively low status, the image of sheet flooring has been transformed with the introduction of new and innovative products. Linoleum is available in an assortment of patterns and colors (usually hessian-backed), and have the added appeal of being relatively eco-friendly. Synthetic rubber is also available in brilliant contemporary colors and a wide range of textures, and offers a great option for walls and floors. Vinyl has also shaken off its rather frumpy image. By incorporating images beneath a clear durable surface, vinyls can offer the effect of natural finishes, such as marble and wood, but in a more practical format. These durable surfaces will look and feel synthetic, but are cheap, effective, and easy to maintain. More recently, the use of digital technology has produced rather more tongue-in-cheek graphics offering abstract and bold images which don't take themselves too seriously and are often more successful.

Laminates involve a similar process, either using a thin layer of a natural material or a photographic representation. Almost any image can now be used to create high-performance panels. Some laminates are available with slight relief effects, such as quilted copper. Whatever the choice, laminates deliver high-performance sheets for walls and work surfaces.

In addition to sheet materials, some synthetics can be made to measure, shaped to form integral features and molded recesses for appliances. Structural and decorative, there are limitless possibilities. Plastic is also a malleable material (and relatively inexpensive) and can be shaped and molded in any fashion. Acrylic or polycarbonate sheets are rigid, transparent, or opaque, and are ideal for use as splashbacks or lightweight screens. Recycled plastic can be reformed into panels for use on worktops or walls.

Composite materials formed from crushed minerals are another alternative, offering smooth hardwearing surfaces that are also highly versatile. Corian®, for example, with its seamless surface and satin sheen finish which becomes more silken with use, is a popular choice. Even derivatives of concrete can be dyed and formed into precast seamless surfaces or machine-cut into tiles and slabs.

Some of these products have been around a long time, but with the development of modern materials and manufacturing techniques, synthetics have entered a new era. The majority are easy to install, durable, and low maintenance. Despite being precision-engineered and brightly colored, of nonstandard textures, and offering high performance, they are nonetheless available at affordable prices. They also retain color well and won't fade over time. The drawback is that they lack the cachet that comes with history and will never develop that charming patina which some find so appealing on aged materials.

11.1 Processed Naturals

Made entirely from natural materials, linoleum offers a practical, hardwearing alternative to more expensive surfaces and a soft feel underfoot. For the more adventurous, rubber flooring can cover vast areas with vivid color and exciting textures, combining style with value for money. Decorative laminates, formed from natural materials such as wood, metal, and paper, provide your interior with smooth, cost-effective, easy-maintenance surfaces.

SPECIFICATIONS

■ **Size:**

Lino: Sheets or tiles, sizes vary depending on maufacturer.
Rubber: Sheets, tiles, or rolls, sizes vary depending on manufacturer.
Laminates: Sheets, size varies depending on manufacturer.

■ **Surface texture:**

Lino: Generally smooth, consistent thickness with a degree of cushioning.
Rubber: Smooth or textured, high shine or matte, consistent thickness, seamless effect, warm and tactile underfoot. Softer rubbers can be used in similar ways to textiles.
Laminate: Flat or textured.

■ **Colors:**

Lino: Over 100 available.
Rubber: Many clear vivid colors; holds pigment well.
Laminates: Extensive range.

■ **Finish:**

Lino: Matte, shiny.
Rubber: Naturally matte, slip-resistant, and antistatic.
Laminates: Matte, gloss.

■ **Applications:**

Lino: Flooring.
Rubber: Flooring, matting, walls, upholstery, furnishings.
Laminates: Countertops, cupboards, interior wall cladding, flooring.

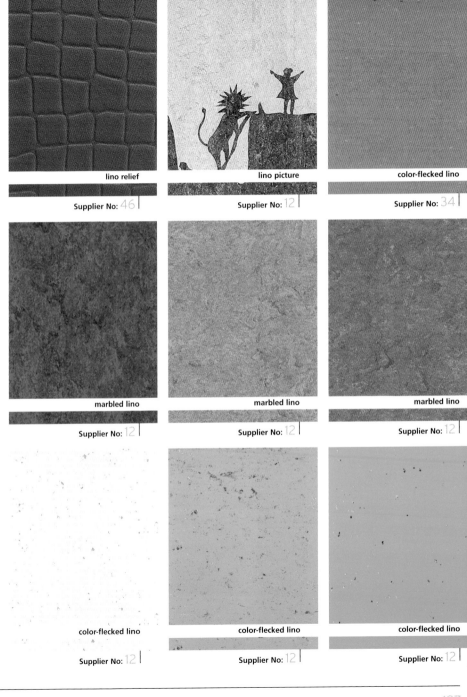

lino relief

Supplier No: 46

lino picture

Supplier No: 12

color-flecked lino

Supplier No: 34

marbled lino

Supplier No: 12

marbled lino

Supplier No: 12

marbled lino

Supplier No: 12

color-flecked lino

Supplier No: 12

color-flecked lino

Supplier No: 12

color-flecked lino

Supplier No: 12

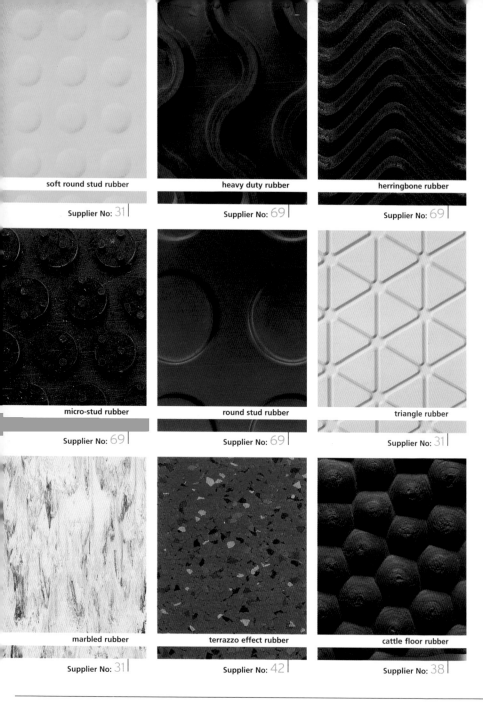

soft round stud rubber

Supplier No: 31

heavy duty rubber

Supplier No: 69

herringbone rubber

Supplier No: 69

micro-stud rubber

Supplier No: 69

round stud rubber

Supplier No: 69

triangle rubber

Supplier No: 31

marbled rubber

Supplier No: 31

terrazzo effect rubber

Supplier No: 42

cattle floor rubber

Supplier No: 38

New technology has allowed decorative laminate manufacturers to develop new ranges of high-performance panels of real wood veneers and metal foils, fused at high temperatures into a solid laminated core. Available in a large-sheet format, these panels need no finishing, are easy to maintain, and can be more durable than the real thing.

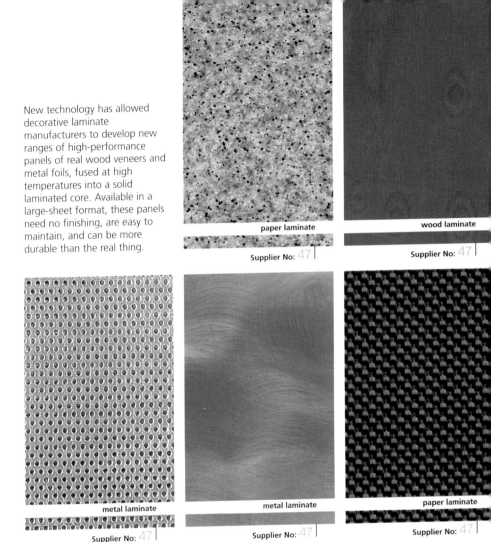

paper laminate
Supplier No: 47

wood laminate
Supplier No: 47

metal laminate
Supplier No: 47

metal laminate
Supplier No: 47

paper laminate
Supplier No: 47

BUYER INFORMATION

Linoleum finishes tend to be high-performance, sound-absorbing, and extremely durable (a 25-year life span is not unusual). Lino is fire-resistant, antistatic, and antibacterial. When properly sealed it is water- and flame-resistant.

Rubber flooring is durable, antistatic, water- and flame-resistant and provides good sound insulation. It can be purchased in a variety of forms: plain to terrazzo effect, or studded and textured. Textured rubber is antislip, making it ideal for bathrooms. However, the textures can attract dirt so should be cleaned regularly.

11.2 Synthetics

Vinyl is a popular flooring product which, although not cheap, is easy to maintain and relatively hardwearing. Heat-seaming gives a continuous and impervious, wipe-clean, watertight finish.
Acrylic sheeting is an extremely versatile and lightweight solution, offering durability and creative potential for cupboard doors, countertops, splashbacks, and light-transmitting window screens.

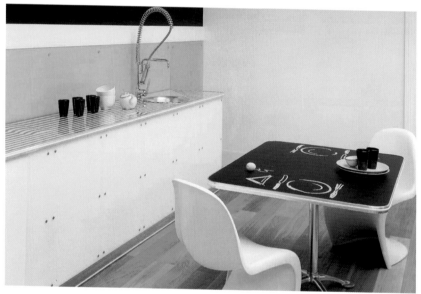

SPECIFICATIONS

■ Size:
Vinyl: Sheet and tile sizes vary depending upon manfacturer.
Acrylic: Sheet typically 120 x 80 in. (3050 x 2030mm), ⅛–½ in. (3–12mm) thick.

■ Surface texture:
Vinyl: Flat, smooth, textured, matte, consistent.
Acrylic: Flat, diamond, ripple, stipple.

■ Colors:
Full spectrum.

■ Finish:
Vinyl: Abrasion- and slip-resistant, tough clear 0.9mm vinyl wear layer, comfortable underfoot.
Acrylic: Gloss, silk, matte, frost, pearlescent, clear, translucent, tinted, opaque.

■ Options:
Vinyl: Bespoke design service.
Acrylic: Available in specialist resilient and fire-resistant stronger formats.

■ Applications:
Vinyl: Unique and wide-ranging; suitable for areas of heavy wear, commercial and domestic; a good choice for areas of higher condensation.
Acrylic: Splashbacks, feature walls, doors, window screens, shelves.

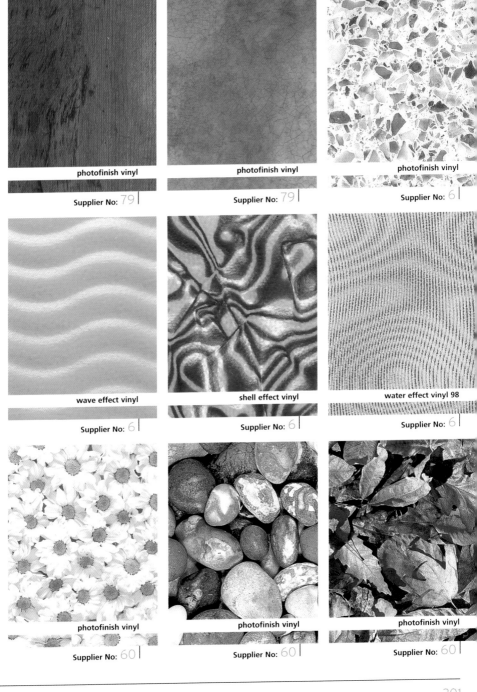

photofinish vinyl

Supplier No: 79

photofinish vinyl

Supplier No: 79

photofinish vinyl

Supplier No: 6

wave effect vinyl

Supplier No: 6

shell effect vinyl

Supplier No: 6

water effect vinyl 98

Supplier No: 6

photofinish vinyl

Supplier No: 60

photofinish vinyl

Supplier No: 60

photofinish vinyl

Supplier No: 60

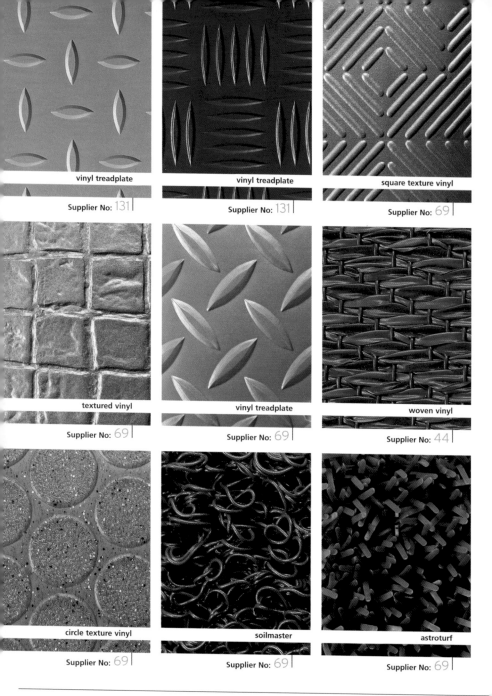

vinyl treadplate

Supplier No: 131

vinyl treadplate

Supplier No: 131

square texture vinyl

Supplier No: 69

textured vinyl

Supplier No: 69

vinyl treadplate

Supplier No: 69

woven vinyl

Supplier No: 44

circle texture vinyl

Supplier No: 69

soilmaster

Supplier No: 69

astroturf

Supplier No: 69

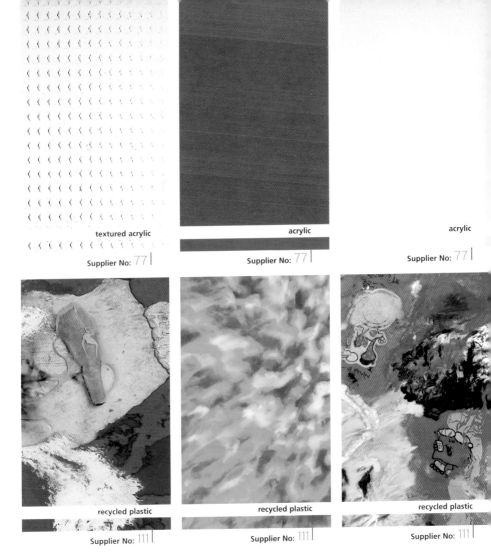

textured acrylic

Supplier No: 77

acrylic

Supplier No: 77

acrylic

Supplier No: 77

recycled plastic

Supplier No: 111

recycled plastic

Supplier No: 111

recycled plastic

Supplier No: 111

BUYER INFORMATION
Vinyl can cost the equivalent of some natural alternatives, so it isn't just a cheap option.
Digital technology means companies now offer a bespoke service for individual layouts.
Acrylic sheeting is available in a variety of finishes: laser-cut, shaped, milled, drilled,
thermoformed, polished, screen-printed, and engraved.
Relatively new to the market, but growing in popularity and function, recycled plastics
can be formed into pliable multicolored sheets from everyday objects, such as cellphones
and toothbrushes.

11.3 Faux

There are many high-quality artificial floor and wall finishes available that emulate natural materials with varying degrees of authenticity. Although not as tactile, there can be benefits. Faux finishes are lighter and more flexible, and can be applied to a variety of surfaces without timely preparation, so are a good choice where cost and weight are prohibitive.

SPECIFICATIONS

■ **Size:**
Tile and sheet sizes vary depending on manufacturer.

■ **Surface texture:**
Embossed and punched textures, combine gloss and matte, smooth or textured.

■ **Colors:**
Many available.

■ **Finish:**
Wax or polyurethane; matte or shiny.

■ **Options:**
Splashbacks, benchtops, feature walls, doors, window screens, shelves.

■ **Applications:**
Bespoke design service; solid core; laminates colored throughout.

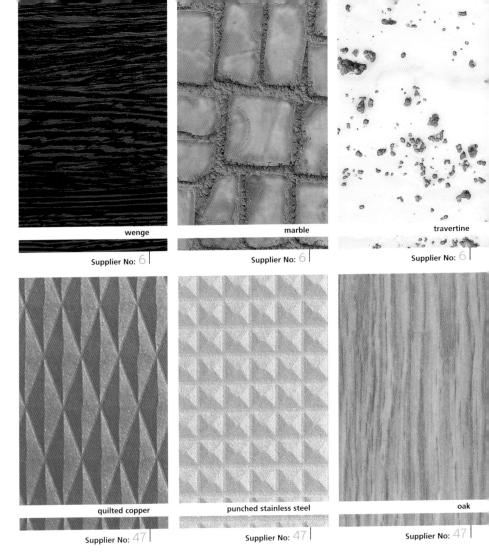

wenge

Supplier No: 6

marble

Supplier No: 6

travertine

Supplier No: 6

quilted copper

Supplier No: 47

punched stainless steel

Supplier No: 47

oak

Supplier No: 47

BUYER INFORMATION

Fakes can offer increased performance over the real thing, with easy-to-clean, hardwearing, and stain-resistant surfaces. Laminates are easy to maintain and won't fade in direct sunlight. They can be installed over most types of floor or wall substrate, and are great for countertops. Laminate and vinyl are easy to self-install and transport, and manufacture costs can be less than for quarried materials, such as stone. If irony is your choice they can also be found in an array of unconvincing colors.

11.4 Precast & Composite

Composite products offer hardwearing, nonporous surfaces. They are formed from various materials, including natural minerals, marble, quartz, and glass, and are chemically bonded to produce a high-performance, ultrasmooth surface. Composites are durable, renewable, and can can be shaped, molded, cut, carved, or sandblasted. Alternatively, laminated concrete work surfaces are also solid and are available in a range of unusual colors and aggregates.

SPECIFICATIONS

■ Size:
Tiles, slabs, sizes vary; or made to measure, thermoformed, drilled, cut, carved to suit.

■ Surface texture:
Solid, smooth.

■ Colors:
Myriad of colors, glass and quartz content adds sparkle.

■ Finish:
Ultrasmooth polished finish, high gloss, matte, satin sheen.

■ Options:
Bespoke design service available.

■ Applications:
Countertops, integrated kitchen and bathroom products, flooring and cladding, bespoke furniture.

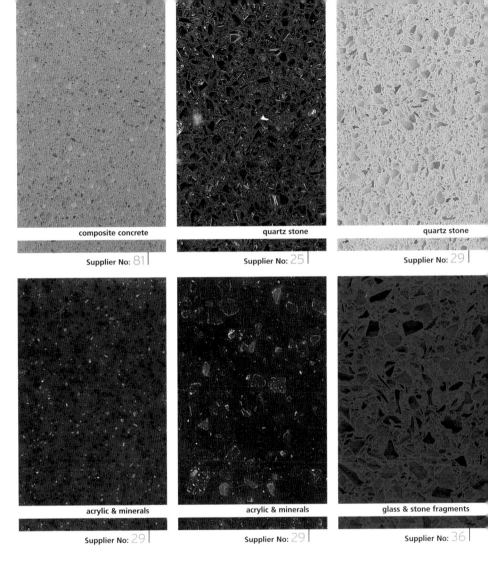

composite concrete

Supplier No: 81

quartz stone

Supplier No: 25

quartz stone

Supplier No: 29

acrylic & minerals

Supplier No: 29

acrylic & minerals

Supplier No: 29

glass & stone fragments

Supplier No: 36

BUYER INFORMATION

Many companies offer a bespoke design service, casting large surface areas without seams, and incorporating spaces for sinks and hobs. Sinks can even be molded to your specifications. Composite surfaces are nonporous, hygenic, and stain-resistant. Composite concrete is priced similar to granite and some quartz and mineral composites. Factory-cast, durable, and relatively lightweight, sheets are presealed for immediate use. Finishes are bold, versatile, and provide a reliable alternative to natural stone.

12 Site Surfaces

Site surfaces comprise *in situ* finishes for floors, walls, and worktops with a no-frills industrial aesthetic. While debate continues over their aesthetic appeal, their practical and hardwearing qualities, coupled with their versatility, mean site surfaces are increasingly being used for domestic interiors.

Aesthetics

If you want nonbranded textural interiors, then look no further than concrete and plaster. Typically concealed by additional surface finishes, both materials can be left raw and exposed. Simple and austere, they provide an unassuming backdrop for the surrounding accessories of any interior. Plaster can be polished smooth to a luminous shine or left soft, chalky, and uneven, but either way, it provides a more interesting texture than plain paper or paint. Ecologically sound and easy-to-use, pigments can be added to the clay to introduce color. Concrete uses similar natural and inexpensive ingredients. When used outside, it can appear brutal and aggressive, but when used inside, it becomes surprisingly self-effacing. Concrete takes itself rather seriously, and if used extensively, the resulting appearance is no longer understated and "image-free," but instead will glorify the mundane to spectacular effect.

Plaster is usually troweled on, but there are other textured finishes that can be brushed on and then finished to provide a consistent three-dimensional look. Generally considered to be rather tasteless, these textured finishes are more durable than paints or vinyl wallpapers, so with careful selection, the rugged surfaces will conceal imperfections with a degree of style. Alternatively, if you prefer ironic interiors, then there are plenty of them to choose from.

Commercial floors are increasingly being used in domestic interiors, and industrial-strength glamor is available in shiny, seamless, multicolored resin floors. Sleek and durable, the clean lines, immaculate uniformity, and powerful reflective colors are in stark contrast to irregular matte finishes such as wood or stone. These poured floors are minimalist and robust. Available as gloss or matte, textural effects can be created by adding flakes or even glitter to the color base. Unique and fluid artworks are also possible with poured polypropylene (available in specialist colors and designs made to order), a pigmented coating, or the integration of images under a clear resin binder. You can now create effects such as marble over extensive surfaces that are seamless and soft underfoot.

A blend of the natural and synthetic, terrazzo is generally considered a more luxurious finish. Decorative patterns and a seamless surface are created with variegated chips of glass, marble, or granite embedded in concrete cement- or resin-based material. Cool underfoot and with limitless combinations of colors and aggregate, terrazzo floors achieve a fabulous sense of depth. Chipped stone is another such option: rugged underfoot, this tactile flooring is available in a range of colors.

The following surfaces are typically applied and worked on-site in a wet state and left to cure. *In situ* finishes offer plenty of opportunities for an industrially hard aesthetic and unadorned interiors, but there is scope also for the practical and the decorative with unique surfaces that are rich in texture, depth, and warmth.

12.1 Plastered

Traditionally concealed under paint or wall coverings, exposed plaster has now established its identity as a striking finish. The delicate texture and typically neutral tones provide an unobtrusive backdrop, but it is far more versatile than expected: waxed and polished to a slight sheen gives an interesting luminosity while glitter, sand, or even straw can be added to the mix or rubbed into the finished surface to provide color and texture. The surface can also be manipulated into patterns when wet, and embellished with moldings or decorations.

SPECIFICATIONS

■ **Size:**
Varies; trowel on *in-situ*. Under- and topcoats or one-coat plaster available.

■ **Surface texture:**
Smooth or textured, and embellished with moldings or decoration.

■ **Colors:**
Typically pinkish-brown, gray, or off-white, but added pigments create unusual colors.

■ **Finish:**
Sealed with matte varnish or wax (this darkens color); polish to a slight sheen.

■ **Applications:**
Walls, ceilings.

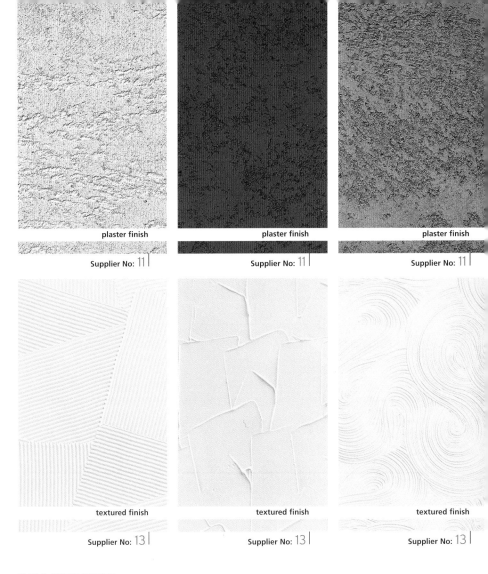

plaster finish

Supplier No: 11

plaster finish

Supplier No: 11

plaster finish

Supplier No: 11

textured finish

Supplier No: 13

textured finish

Supplier No: 13

textured finish

Supplier No: 13

BUYER INFORMATION
Economical and relatively easy to apply, plaster can be used to hide other defects. Ranges of rendered finishes, applied to rough walls and patterned when wet, can create relief finishes and sculptural effects. Often discarded as old-fashioned, they do smooth over unsightly defects in any surface, but do require a degree of skilled application, and if mistakes are made, can be difficult to remove without damaging the surface below. Plaster is soft and porous so should be sealed. Plaster finishes can be applied to flat or curved surfaces. To retain straight corner details, apply metal corner beads before plastering.

12.2 Poured

With an industrial aesthetic and seamless finish, poured epoxy-based resin floors are typically chemical- and scratch-resistant, easy to maintain, hygienic, and nonslip. Available in high gloss or matte, the color and texture can offer dramatic effect. Images can be bound into the floor and fixed with a durable epoxy seal. Granulated finishes like stone carpet, where natural and synthetic aggregates and stones are bound with clear epoxy resin, offer versatile and dynamic flooring of different grades of finish. Terrazzo, used for centuries in domestic interiors, enjoys a more sophisticated image than other industrial-strength floors. The mix of natural stone, marble, colored glass chips, concrete, or cement results in an infinite range of patterns.

SPECIFICATIONS

■ **Size:**
Terrazzo: Usually poured *in-situ*, applied with trowel and cured. From ⅟₁₆–⅜ in. (2–10mm) thick.
Resin: Typically ⅟₁₆–⅜ in. (2–10mm), but ⅗₁₆ (15mm) is possible.

■ **Surface texture:**
Terrazzo: Appearance varies according to mix and size of aggregate—fine to clumpy, large chips for mottled effect.
Resin: Smooth, lightly textured.

■ **Colors:**
Terrazzo: Many background colors and marble chip colors.
Resin: A wide range of solid colors, but color flakes can be added.

■ **Finish:**
Terrazzo: Ground smooth and polished; dividing strips made of brass or zinc.
Resin: Smooth, seamless, or textured, matte or gloss coatings.

■ **Applications:**
Terrazzo: Mainly used for flooring, countertops, stairs, furniture.
Resin: Flooring.

multiscreed resin

Supplier No: 4

multiscreed resin

Supplier No: 4

pebblestone resin

Supplier No: 4

pebblestone resin

Supplier No: 4

natural stone resin

Supplier No: 68

marble resin

Supplier No: 68

stone carpet

Supplier No: 32

quartz resin

Supplier No: 68

glitter resin

Supplier No: 68

textured terrazzo

Supplier No: 97

resin based terrazzo

Supplier No: 4

textured terrazzo

Supplier No: 97

textured terrazzo

Supplier No: 97

patterned terrazzo

Supplier No: 94

resin terrazzo

Supplier No: 50

resin terrazzo

Supplier No: 50

resin terrazzo

Supplier No: 50

resin terrazzo

Supplier No: 50

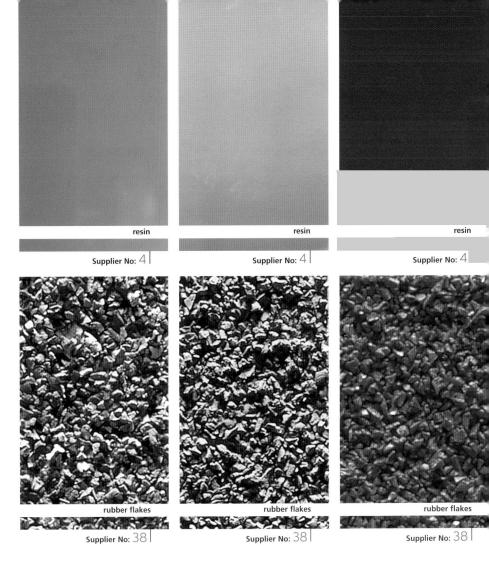

resin

Supplier No: 4

resin

Supplier No: 4

resin

Supplier No: 4

rubber flakes

Supplier No: 38

rubber flakes

Supplier No: 38

rubber flakes

Supplier No: 38

BUYER INFORMATION

Poured floors are extremely durable, so offer good value for money, but terrazzo flooring is labor-intensive and therefore not cheap. Terrazzo can also be purchased in tile form.

Specialist contractors usually install *in-situ* floors, but the finished effect is only as good as the subfloor, which must be carefully prepared to get a seamless finish.

Textured finishes, of stone or rubber, are tactile underfoot and great when combined with underfloor heating; providing a decorative alternative to concrete, it has good sound absorbency. Some manufacturers allow a choice of base color and flake mix to be tailored to your specification, so glitter and color can be added to suit.

12.3 Finishes

Concrete is often considered austere but photo-etching can add graphics and pigments can produce many colors. It can also be treated after curing—hammer, paint, stain, or inlays added when wet—to interesting effect. Specialist plaster finishes—stucco, gesso, fresco, scagliola, marmorino—combine pigments, oils, wax, and metallic and marble dust. Finishes are applied in layers to create textures from ultrasmooth, polished surfaces to faux stone.

SPECIFICATIONS

■ **Size:**
Concrete: Preformed off-site as slabs, tiles, or pavers; or site-cast and molded into a variety of shapes.
Plaster: Varies; trowel on *in-situ*.

■ **Surface texture:**
Concrete: Pleasing irregularity in texture, color, and thicknesses; can be sandblasted and etched to create patterns.
Plaster: Smooth or textured.

■ **Colors:**
Concrete: Typically gray, but there is a huge difference between cast and polished surfaces; dyes can be added.
Plaster: Typically pinkish-brown, gray, or off-white, but can be colored.

■ **Finish:**
Concrete: Dries to a suede-like appearance; polished, unpolished; cast concrete is an even light gray; polishing removes top layer to expose sand and aggregate; appearance depends on aggregate, polished or matte; inlays.
Plaster: Sealed, polished, waxed.

■ **Applications:**
Concrete: Custom-molded benchtops, furniture, walls, flooring.
Plaster: Walls, ceilings.

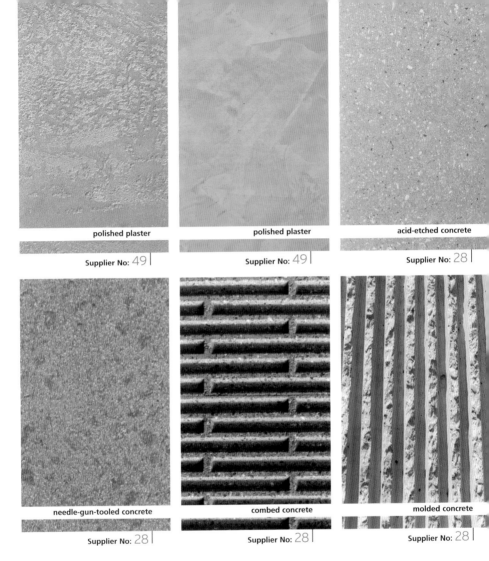

polished plaster

Supplier No: 49

polished plaster

Supplier No: 49

acid-etched concrete

Supplier No: 28

needle-gun-tooled concrete

Supplier No: 28

combed concrete

Supplier No: 28

molded concrete

Supplier No: 28

BUYER INFORMATION

The basic components of concrete (water, sand, granite, and cement) are inexpensive but can be labor-intensive to install. A good conductor of heat, it's a good choice for underfloor heating. Polishing and sealing gives the most practical surface.

Ornamental plaster finishes are often extremely labor-intensive and therefore are costly. Specially formulated plasters are usually custom made.

Practical Advice

The properties of your chosen materials not only control appearance, but also installation, performance, and durability. Consider the aesthetics, function, practicalities, maintenance, durability, availability, and the purchase and installation costs before making a choice.

Carpets & Rugs

PRACTICAL ADVICE

- *Carpets.* Consider type of room, size, shape, pile height and weight before making any choice.
  There are two main ways to make carpet—tufting and weaving. Tufted carpets are created by stitching the pile yarns through a backing material, usually synthetic, before a backing layer, often jute, is fixed for greater strength. Woven carpets are more dimensionally stable because the pile-face is woven with integral backing. Wearability depends upon pile weight. A carpet with a heavier pile weight will be more durable. Color batches will vary between rolls of different pile weights, so it is advisable to use the same pile weight throughout.
  Choose your pile carefully; for example, velvet pile will show footmarks more readily than twist pile, so it is not practical for some applications.
- *Natural matting.* Subject to color variations and displays varying quantities of knots and other minor imperfections caused by manufacture.

INSTALLATION

- Floor surfaces must be correctly prepared for the material being laid, furniture removed, and appliances unplugged.
- *Carpets.* Can be cut to any size, but check roll width to ensure required coverage. A good-quality underlay will protect against daily wear-and-tear.

- *Natural matting.* Fitting is not straightforward; refer to supplier for specialist advice. To reduce the risk of shrinkage, natural flooring should be allowed to acclimatize to the ambient temperature and humidity of the room for 48 hours prior to fitting. Some manufacturers advise that underlay can increase wear on matting and recommend instead that it should be glued directly onto a smooth dry subfloor.
- *Rugs.* To reduce curling, roll in the opposite direction to the way presented and leave for 24 hours. Double-sided tape will help keep rugs flat and prevent lateral movement.

MAINTENANCE

- *Carpets.* Vacuum often to prevent dirt becoming ingrained; mop spills from edge inward. Follow manufacturers' instructions. All carpets become scruffy, but small areas are fairly easy to replace.
- *Natural matting.* Hides dirt well, but vacuum regularly. Doormats help prevent tracking of dirt. Stains can be hard to remove so pretreat with a stain inhibitor. Refer to supplier advice but generally stains should be blotted with a clean, damp cloth; do not use soap and water or carpet cleaner. It is possible to spray rush with water, but sisal, coir, or jute should never be soaked. As with any natural fiber, direct sunlight may affect the color.

2 Paint

PRACTICAL ADVICE

- Modern paints are water- or oil-based, and vary enormously in quality.
- Select the right paint for the surface, for example, washable vinyl for high-maintenance areas.
- Don't rely on paint swatches. Variations in light can dramatically alter the final effect so buy sample pots and test in a number of areas in the room.
- Follow manufacturers' recommendations to calculate coverage. Paint is made in batches, so colors or consistency may vary between batches. If mixing to order then buy extra paint as later batches might vary in color.
- Properties vary widely between makes, so follow manufacturers' instructions, but the following serves as a basic guide.
  - —*Floors*: Eggshell, satinwood, and gloss; apply specialist floor paint on concrete, stone, brick, wood.
  - —*Furniture:* Eggshell, satinwood, gloss, dead-flat oil, melamine paint.
  - —*Kitchens and bathrooms:* Eggshell, semi-matte or silk emulsion, specialist paint.
  - —*Walls and ceilings:* Matte, metallic, or silk emulsion; eggshell; use limewash for a chalky glazed finish.
  - —*Washable surfaces:* Silk emulsions; use eggshell or semi-matte emulsion for a tougher finish.
  - —*Woodwork (external):* Exterior gloss or eggshell.
  - —*Woodwork (internal):* Dead-flat oil, eggshell, satinwood, gloss.

INSTALLATION

- Patience and a properly prepared surface are essential. Remove old paint; fill and sand holes; wash walls with a sugar and soap solution; wash and sand wood to provide key surface for paint; treat surfaces with primer, undercoat, and topcoat. Corresponding base coats are generally available for all finishes.
- Paint gloss before emulsion (emulsion drips are easier to clean off) and ceilings first, then cornices, shelves, doors, windows, and walls.
- Scumble glaze is suitable for walls, floors, and furniture, but ensure surfaces are consistently smooth to create an even finish, and seal with protective varnish.

MAINTENANCE

- Paint surface can be wiped clean with a damp cloth or with household cleaning products for more stubborn stains.
- Priming new surfaces assists in stain removability.

Paper

PRACTICAL ADVICE

- Paper is a good way to conceal imperfections; for the best effect lining paper should be used.
- Wallpaper backings vary widely and will affect the paper's suitability for particular applications. Always check the attributes of the paper before you purchase.
- Specialist papers are often not suitable for damp areas as some (e.g. grasscloth) will mark easily.
- Vinyl-coated paper is wipeable and suited to most areas.
- Color and pattern can vary between batches. Check the batch numbers on the rolls before you purchase.

INSTALLATION

- Walls should be stripped and dry. Any holes and cracks should be filled and smoothed before new paper is applied.
- Most wallpapers have a pattern repeat. Before hanging, refer to the manufacturers' instruction.

MAINTENANCE

- Standard papers can usually be wiped cleaned with a damp sponge.
- Specialist papers are harder to clean, so should be hung where they are less likely to become dirty; always follow manufacturers' instructions.

How to hang wallpaper

1 Measure floor-to-ceiling height and add 3 in. (10cm) to allow for trimming.
2 Use a plumb line to ensure that your first strip is hanging straight.
3 Measure and cut each piece of paper, lay right-side down on a clean worktable.
4 Mix the paste according to the packet's instructions. Brush the paste onto the paper, from the center to the edge.
5 Fold the paper with paste facing inward and carry to the wall.
6 Hang the paper, leaving enough overlap at the top for trimming.
7 Brush the paper with the hanging brush, using long, firm brushstrokes from the center of the paper to the edges.
8 Trim top and bottom of the wallpaper.
9 Roll the seams with a boxwood roller, using a sheet of paper to absorb any excess paste.

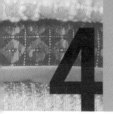

4 Textiles

PRACTICAL ADVICE

- On printed fabrics, pattern and width repeats may vary between batches. Tension may vary on woven fabrics. Color variation between batches is also possible.
- Choose a textile that is suited to the application; not all fabrics are equally suited to loose covers, accessories, upholstery, and curtains. Feel the weight and quality of the fabric before buying.
- Showrooms have a wide range of fabrics, but these are not always all on show; ask if you can't find what you want. Request samples.
- When ordering a specific fabric, check if it can be pretreated for stains, or if fire-retardant is necessary. Remember to add a little to the order to accommodate tolerance. The supplier can advise.
- Natural fabrics tend to fade over time. Before purchase, consider whether they will be in direct sunlight.
- Lined curtains will fall straighter and will offer increased protection from fading. Dry-cleaning will avoid shrinkage.

MAINTENANCE

- Most textiles have a tendency to shrink or pucker. Refer to manufacturers' recommendations, but generally vacuum, wash, or dry-clean. Remove spills immediately.
- Remove linings to avoid differential shrinkage and clean coordinating items at the same time. Most fabrics will shrink a little (3 percent) if dry-cleaned.

- Materials with a slight texture show less wear-and-tear, while synthetics have invaluable wipe-clean properties and are easy to maintain.
- *Synthetics.* These often have wipe-clean, vacuum, or clean periodically instructions; some can be machine-washed, but others may need to be dry-cleaned.
- *Upholstery.* Textiles may fade under direct sunlight. Don't leave furniture in direct contact with a heat source. Turn cushions to even out fading. Arms or seats on furniture wear more easily.
- *Ironing.* Synthetic fabrics should be ironed with a cool iron. Printed cottons and cotton/linen mixes should be ironed on the reverse side, with a medium iron. Glazed chintz should be ironed on the chintz side, with a cool, dry iron.

5

Leather

PRACTICAL ADVICE

- Bear in mind that every hide is unique and that there are huge differences in the handle and feel.
- Not generally available in high street haberdashers, but specialist shops tend to have a huge choice of forms and finishes. Assess the comparative values of leather in terms of its quality. The balance between comfort and durability varies widely, so ensure your choice is suited to its purpose. The supplier will advise.
- Most leathers will be pretested, but check visual and physical characteristics: thickness, quality of finish, accuracy, fastness of color, and flexing endurance.
- Leather is a natural product so expect some variations in color and texture between skins. Samples should be used as a guide only. Genuine leather always displays natural characteristics. such as wrinkles and scratches.

INSTALLATION

- Leather floor tiles must be applied to a dry, level surface (boarded out with ply or hardboard). Use a contact adhesive to fix. Variations will occur between batches, so blend the tiles before fixing.
- Although expensive, leather tiles are relatively easy to install.

MAINTENANCE

- Protect from direct sunlight as color may fade, and or excessive heat which may cause the leather to dry out and crack.

- Some skins are machine-washable and water-repellent, but check for manufacturers' specialist cleaning instructions.
- *Leather*. Periodic maintenance required. Check manufacturers' instructions, but most can be dusted regularly and/or wiped with a soft damp cloth. Leather cream can be used to prevent cracking and to protect against stains, but apply evenly and sparingly. For stubborn stains, seek specialist advice. Cleaners and conditioners will keep leather attractive, supple, and resistant to soiling. Be aware these products can cause color change. The products are generally not for use on suede or nubuck. Do not use oils or furniture polishes because they may contain solvents that can damage the leather.
- *Leather tiling*. Buff floors every few weeks and wax twice a year. Gaps between tiles need to be periodically waxed and buffed, and if properly maintained, the floor should be extremely durable. Spills and marks can be wiped clean or blended into the surface.
- *Suede*. Protect against water and stains using specialist products (usually a spray; test on a small area prior to use). Can also be gently wiped with a clean damp cloth, and the pile renewed using a suede brush or block.

6 Wood

PRACTICAL ADVICE

- Consider aesthetics, practicality, budget, and location. Narrow strips are generally cheaper than wide boards. Hardwood laminates bonded to softwood plank may not be the real thing, but are an economical option.
- Add 10 percent to an order to allow for cutting/wastage.

INSTALLATION

- Always refer to supplier recommendations.
- Manufactured flooring strips are easier to install than solid timber, which may require professional assistance.
- Ensure the site avoids extreme variations of heat or moisture as boards will either shrink or distort.
- All new timber must be seasoned before use.
- Carefully prepare a suitable subfloor (concrete, joists, battens, floorboards, chipboard) for proposed material. Lay a vapor barrier above subfloor; do not use polythene as it may cause timber to sweat. Leave expansion gaps at perimeters (depends on type of board and humidity of room).
- *Blocks.* Bond to the subfloor; do not lay over joists or battens. Fill, sand, and seal after installation.
- *Cork.* Allow to acclimatize for 48 hours before laying on top of suitable subfloor (timber, hardboard, ply). Minor variations in color, so blend tiles before fixing.
- *Decorative finishes.* Manufacturers generally recommend surfaces are

sanded and cleaned prior to application.
- *Floating floor.* Wooden floors are noisy underfoot, but significant sound reduction qualities can be achieved between floors if a hardwood top layer is laid over an acoustic blanket and subfloor to specialist detail. Do not nail through to joists/battens below.
- *Floor painting/staining.* An easy application. Sand back to expose the original wood grain, remove all dust and apply three coats of durable paint. Seal and polish once dry.
- *MDF.* Always wear a mask when working.
- *Chipboard.* Edges should not be exposed as they readily absorb water.
- *Processed boards.* In wet areas, use boards that have been treated with a water repellant.
- *Solid wood strips.* Can be unfinished or prefinished, laid directly over joists, tongued and grooved, sanded and sealed after installation. If fitting multiwidth boards, be sure to blend sizes evenly across the floor.
- *Timber floors.* Sand and clean off any dust before applying a sealer of oil or lacquer.
- *Veneer.* Bookmatch to ensure an even pattern across the surface. Edge any exposed edges (such as nosings to veneered shelves) in solid wood to match.

MAINTENANCE

- Sweep regularly, wipe with a damp mop.
- Direct sunlight can alter the appearance and fade the grain.
- Unstained wood veneers and dyed woods can now be pressure-treated in a vacuum to inhibit fading.
- *Cane.* Splits easily and then is almost impossible to mend. Clean by wiping with water or a solution of washing up liquid. If soaked, allow to dry naturally.
- *Cork.* Sweep regularly and clean with a damp mop. A range of cleaners will suit. Durability depends on the surface seal and extent of traffic, not the thickness of the cork, so apply additional coats of varnish in bathrooms and do not allow surface to wear through first. Use a hard wax finish for light-traffic areas; high-traffic areas can be sealed with a tougher polyurethane varnish.
- *Laminates.* Low maintenance and easy to clean; simply wipe with a damp cloth. Beware of burns, heel or furniture marks because once damaged, repair is difficult—marks can be sanded out but not to the extent of a real floor.
- *Oiled floors.* Oil offers no protection against chemicals or scuff marks. Reoil every three years. Clean using a low pH cleaner, then buff.
- *Reclaimed wood.* Ensure that wood is rot and pest-free. Strip all layers of paint/varnish, patch, and fill.
- *Softwood.* Treat against rot and woodworm before use.
- *Stained floors.* Damaged surfaces can be sanded off and the floor restained.
- *Varnish/lacquer.* Varnish can be extremely durable with a multicoat application. Lacquer is very low maintenance.
- *Waxed floors.* Require regular polishing and rewaxing. Can be cleaned using a mild agent.
- *Work surfaces.* Minor burns can be sanded out. Varnish or oil regularly.
- *Bamboo.* Vacuum with hardwood floor attachments or use a soft brush and wipe with a damp cloth. Do not wax or polish.

7

Stone

PRACTICAL ADVICE

- Select the right material for the job, to provide the required finish and retain structural integrity.
- Nonstandard dimensions are often available on direct request. Hard templates provide a greater degree of accuracy.
- Structural integrity can be impaired by cut-outs.
- A honed finish where the surface may become wet is not recommended. Adding nonslip inserts, grit-blasted strips or grooves can increase slip resistance.
- Flaming isn't recommended for floors as the surface film wears quickly.
- Allow for wastage when ordering stone as minor damage may occur in transit or on site.

INSTALLATION

- Unless you are an expert, don't try to install stone yourself; choose a professional.
- Always check suppliers' recommendations on the specification and how to achieve desired effects.
- Lay onto appropriate substrate as recommended (usually a clean, dry surface, free from wax, grease, or oil). Choice of fixing method depends on substrate. Granites, marble, travertine, and limestone are more susceptible to cracking so should be fixed to an MDF or timber substrate, or increased in thickness. In general, bond stone to subbase with silicone base adhesive. Natural slate and

sandstone are hand-riven so thickness may vary from tile to tile. This difference can be accommodated in the adhesive bed.
- Ensure the floor is able to support the weight of the stone, dead loads, and applied loads. You may need to stiffen timber floors.
- Blend tiles before laying. Dampness will affect color, so ensure stone is dry prior to installation to establish true color. Tonal colors vary from batch to batch, so if trying to match a previously laid floor, do not expect color to match.
- Consider the pattern when laying, either staggered joints or regular grids. Movement joints should be decided at design stage and cover existing expansion joints, junctions between different materials, perimeter of floors and door.
- Grout is not usually applied until adhesive has set. In areas of extreme temperature changes, a flexible grout is recommended.
- Sealant will enhance the color of stone, protect from wear, and ease cleaning and maintenance but may also change the appearance of the stone and increase the slip factor.

MAINTENANCE

- Protect exposed edges when handling to avoid damage.
- Protect from weather during installation—heat, rain, or frost may delay curing of adhesion.
- Protect finished floor after installation until all surrounding works are complete. Wet plaster or

paint can be extremely difficult to remove without causing damage.

- Most stones (except the tightest grained polished granites) are sealed before and after grouting to improve appearance, protect against staining, and assist maintenance. The type of sealant depends on the stone. For example, limestone is porous, and should be fully saturated with sealant, but sealant should only be left on nonporous stone for a few seconds. Most suppliers have their own recommended product so follow advice. Sealant needs periodic reapplication. NB: Incorrectly applied sealant is difficult to remove.
- Follow suppliers' advice. Avoid mopping and powerful abrasive detergents but sweep regularly. Wipe up spills immediately with a damp cloth or, if necessary, a neutral detergent.
- *Limestone*. Susceptible to acid and water, it can scratch and stain easily so sealant is necessary. If treated correctly, the stone will remain problem-free. Wipe with a damp cloth.
- *Marble*. Although water-resistant, marble can be damaged by acid/alkaline substances if not protected. Clean using a damp chamois leather cloth and neutral cleaning products only. Will remain bright if sealed and maintained with natural waxes.
- *Granite*. Low-maintenance, wear poses few problems. Use water; never apply polish.

- *Slate*. Can be easily scratched. Clean with neutral detergent and buff with nylon pad.
- *Quartzite*. Not susceptible to frost or atmospheric pollutants and practically impossible to erode.
- *Travertine*. Filler may work loose in time and require ongoing maintenance.

8 Clay

PRACTICAL ADVICE
- Any good home improvement book will provide detailed information on fixing.

TILE INSTALLATION
- Check with the supplier that tile is suitable for its intended purpose.
- You can lay new tiles over an even surface of existing tiles.
- Good subfloor or wall preparation is essential; should always be dry and even.
- Tiles can be applied directly to many wall finishes—paint, paper, plasterboard, and brick. Handmade tiles are more difficult to fix than machine-made tiles. Floor tiles are thicker than wall tiles and less easy to cut.
- Use an appropriate adhesive— heatproof for behind cookers; waterproof for wet areas.
- Tile adhesive should be dry before grouting commences.
- *Ceramic tiles.* The edges can tend to look less crisp than porcelain, so color and quality of grouting makes huge difference to the success of the overall effect.
- *Mosaics.* Usually prestuck onto a flexible mesh backing, or front-faced paper, which is peeled away after tiles are fixed. It can be difficult to fix evenly and line through all grout joints without emphasizing separate sheets. Pebble sheets should be fixed with adhesive onto well-scored mortar, plaster, or grout. Variations in shade, thickness, color to be expected.

- *Terracotta.* Tiles should be presealed with recommended sealant, linseed oil or wax, then grouted and sealed. Be aware that seals will darken the color. Tiles should be well-mixed before installation to allow an even distribution of color.

BRICK INSTALLATION
- Expect variations in color and texture. The technical specifications and properties of brick types vary widely, so be sure to select one that is suitable for the purpose. Performance of the brick is also dependant upon the mortar used.
- Painting brick increases light reflection, but ensure that there are no light-reflecting materials in the wall. If applied to exterior bricks, the paint should be porous to allow the wall to breathe.

MAINTENANCE
- Ceramics are easy to keep clean, but are unlikely to withstand knocks from heavy objects.
- Buy additional tiles to replace any that crack or chip.
- Sweep and mop with mild detergent. Do not polish nonporous tiles. Keep grout clean using mild detergent or whiteners.
- *Brick.* Repointing joints may be required periodically. Coat or seal internal floors to assist cleaning.

9 Glass

PRACTICAL ADVICE
- Safety glass has a high strength/weight ratio so can be manufactured in larger panels than ordinary glass of similar size. However, larger sheets are heavy and can be awkward to manipulate. Glass sheets can be framed or frameless, but exposed edges will need polishing.

INSTALLATION
- Many applications (flooring, decorative glass screens) require specialist design specification, engineering, and installation.
- You cannot drill holes in toughened glass; fixing holes should be drilled before the glass is toughened.
- Ensure the surface finish is suitable for the application: polished glass floors will be slippery and should have sandblasted strips applied for extra grip; mosaics are unsuitable for floors as they become slippery if wet, grout becomes dirty, and they can easily come unstuck if not laid properly; splashbacks should be toughened or laminated to improve heat and impact resistance.
- Some decorative finishes have a preferred viewing side so make sure they are installed correctly: colored glass should be fixed with enameled face to the rear to maximize appearance of depth; acid-etched shower screens or windows lose obscurity when wet, so etch both sides if privacy is required.
- When installing glass tiles, ensure that the adhesive covers the back of the tile evenly. Uneven coverage will be visible through the tile.
- Glass blocks are heavy so the quality and strength of the subfloor is essential.
- Laminated panels are difficult to handle if large, and cannot be drilled once formed. They can be point-fixed top and bottom, or framed into fixed panels or sliding walls.

MAINTENANCE
- Glass is relatively easy to clean, but time-consuming as it will show every finger smudge or water mark. Clean regularly using standard cleaners and lint-free cloths.

10 Metal

PRACTICAL ADVICE

- *Aluminum.* Durable, resistant to corrosion, lightweight, and relatively cheap. Easier to maintain than stainless steel, it won't show every finger mark or scratch. Floor tiles may provide contrast in texture but can be fairly noisy and cold underfoot. Won't shatter.
- *Steel.* Stronger than iron. There are 100 types of steel alloy available, each with different properties.
- *Stainless steel.* Work surfaces are hygienic, heatproof, durable, and can be welded together into seamless units. Color may vary between different batches.
- *Weaves:* Unique characteristics depending on proximity, thickness, and configuration of wire. Various types available, from fine and flexible to rigid welded panels as solid steel plate.
- *Zinc.* Very pliable. Marks easily and dulls over time. Naturally resistant to corrosion.

INSTALLATION

- *Salvaged metal.* Sand off rust with wire wool and seal with matte lacquer. Renew paint finishes.
- *Sheet flooring.* Fix metal floor over level timber or concrete substrate, or weld to a timber base to reduce footfall noise. Stick or screw into place.

MAINTENANCE

- *Brass.* High maintenance. Requires regular polishing to maintain a high shine.

- *Copper.* Tarnishes easily. Although highly durable, displays a familiar green patina when it oxidizes.
- *Steel.* Tends to scratch and show finger marks, so restore to pristine finish using scouring powder, buff, and polish, and protect with an application of baby oil. Bleach may cause corrosion. Stainless steel requires high maintenance as it scratches easily and shows water marks.

Durables

PRACTICAL ADVICE

- Durability varies considerably. Cheaper products are generally less resilient.

INSTALLATION

- All materials should be installed in accordance with manufacturers' instructions. Preparation is vital.
- *Linoleum.* Back with cork for added cushioning and sound insulation. Lay onto an even surface, ¼ in. (6mm) ply. Fill and sand from center (awkward edges will be less visible), trim with steel edge. Tiles may temporarily tint yellow after installation, but this will subside after a few hours of daylight.
- *Rubber.* Leave for 48 hours to acclimatize before applying with a flexible bond to a clean, dry substrate. It is not advisable to install over old coverings such as vinyl. Available in a variety of sheet and tile sizes, accessories include stair nosings and skirtings.
- *Vinyl.* Leave to acclimatize before laying onto a smooth, hard, dry subfloor. Vinyl is flammable so ensure that it is suited to the area. The three basic types of vinyl surface—no-wax, urethane (PVC), and enhanced urethane—offer varying levels of protection. If buying tiles, mix them to ensure minimal variation. If buying on a roll try to cover the surface in one piece. If seams are necessary, consider the pattern match.
- *Technical stone.* Like natural stone, it can be machine cut to suit.

MAINTENANCE

- Maintenance depends on the quality of the material but it is vital to ensure long wear.
- *Corian®.* Through-colored so doesn't erode or delaminate, although heavily pigmented colors require more frequent care. Develops minor abrasion marks with use but scratches can be restored. Impact- and stain-resistant.
- *Laminate.* Rounded edges are less likely to chip but can be restored with repairer. Clean with antibacterial cleaner and protect from excess heat and strong solutions.
- *Linoleum.* Sweep and wash with mild detergent; do not polish. Do not allow water to get in underneath or it will lift.
- *Rubber.* Sweep and mop clean with mild detergent. Polish intensifies color so apply sparingly. Dirt gathers on textured surfaces. Protect from hot items, which may burn into the surface. Easy-to-clean finish. PVC-free quality rubber is chemical- and fire-resistant and dirt-repellent.
- *Vinyl.* Sweep and/or vacuum regularly. Wash with mild soap solution, not solvents. Apply bright acrylic-based polish to maintain original appearance. Black shoe marks can stain permanently.
- *Technical stone.* No wax or sealant is required. Clean using a damp cloth and non-abrasive household cleaner.

Site Surfaces

PRACTICAL ADVICE
- Ensure the materials chosen are suitable for the purpose.

INSTALLATION
- Specialist contractors usually install *in situ* floors, but the finished effect is only as good as the subfloor, which must be carefully prepared to get a seamless finish.
- *Concrete.* Requires a dry substrate. Cure at an even rate for 4 hours–4 weeks; will crack if mixed badly or cured inadequately. Difficult to match with older concrete and is extremely porous, so sealing is important; finish with wax. Can be cast using molds of timber, ply, and steel, but the surface will be imprinted on the finished concrete.
- *Plaster.* Soft and porous; hairline cracks are normal. Seal and use several coats of wax, buffed to finish. Finishes require skilled application and errors can be difficult to remove without damaging the surface below.
- *Polypropylene.* Must be installed over level concrete or screed substrate. Leave to cure/bond 6 hours–7 days. Poured and troweled on. Metal edge trim at joints as required.
- *Resin.* Some use clear sealant. Install over level concrete or screed substrate following manufacturers' recommendations. Cracking likely if substrate is not cured properly. Can be dressed up around stands. Poured and troweled on. Leave to cure/bond 6 hours–7 days.

- *Terrazzo.* Requires level concrete base. Easy to incorporate with underfloor heating.

MAINTENANCE
- *Concrete.* Low maintenance. Extremely durable. Clean with soap and water. Acid/acidic substances and sugar will cause staining.
- *Polypropylene.* Clean with rotary scrubber and a mild alkaline detergent.
- *Resin.* Easy to clean and maintain; hardwearing.
- *Stone carpet.* Vacuum and occasional low-pressure water jet and wet vacuum to remove excess water.
- *Terrazzo.* Polish regularly.

Glossary

CARPETS & RUGS

Abaca Made in the Philippines from banana leaves.

Blended A mix of more than one fiber.

Boucle Looped or curled design.

Coir One of the toughest of the natural matting; made from strong outer husks of coconut, primarily from Kerala, India.

Jute Softer but the least resistant natural matting. Woven from the inner bark of corchorus plants primarily grown in southern India.

Loop pile Yarn looped through the backing of the carpet.

Pile Surface created by the ends of the carpet threads. Can be looped, twisted, cord, cut, velvet, or shag.

Pile density The weight of a pile yarn in a unit volume of carpet. Also called "average pile yarn weight." The closer the tufts are to each other, the denser the pile, the greater the pile density, the greater the wearability of the carpet.

Pile height The length of the tuft from the primary backing to the tip. A carpet with a higher pile height will have more yarn on the surface and will therefore be more durable.

Pile weight The total weight of the face of the carpet.

Seagrass A marine plant grown in China and Vietnam.

Sisal Relatively inexpensive, extracted from African and South American grass; can be woven coarsely or tightly.

Tufted Pile material stitched into an existing backing material before a second layer of backing material is fixed for greater structural strength.

Twist Two or more yarns twisted together to create the carpet. A higher twist level usually results in better texture retention and better resilience.

Underlay Lies underneath the carpet and helps protect it from wear-and-tear.

Woven Pile face that is woven with an integral backing.

PAINT

Acrylic eggshell paint Water-based paint that dries to a smooth silky finish giving a gentle sheen. Gives a tougher, more washable finish than emulsion paint. Can be used for interior woodwork.

Acrylic primer Water-based; used to seal wood and fiberboard.

Acrylics Fast-drying, water-based paints.

Aging Techniques that emulate the effects of time and wear on surfaces.

Base coat First coat to be applied to most decorative paint finishes.

Casein (milk) paint Water-soluble; similar dusty finish to limewash.

Colorwash Water-based; translucent colored glaze.

Color stainer/tinter Concentrated coloring agent.

Combing Decorative technique in which the teeth of a comb are scraped through a surface glaze to reveal the color below.

Crackle glaze/craquelure Traditional glaze created by layering oil- and water-based paints that dry at different speeds, or by rubbing color into a topcoat of varnish; identifiable by its delicate cracks.

Dead flat oil Matte oil-based paint; found in traditional ranges.

Distemper Water-based paint with a powdery finish.

Eggshell Low-sheen finish available in wide range of colors; applied using the same method as gloss paint.

Emulsion Water-based paint usually used for internal walls and ceilings. Vinyl or acrylic resins are now added to make them more hardwearing than traditional finishes.

Glaze Transparent layer of color used over a base coat.

Gloss Hardwearing and washable; available in wide range of colors from most major suppliers.

Limewash Used for tinting porous surfaces such as plaster; gives a translucent finish which dries to a velvety matte finish.

Matte emulsion Water-based paint with a flat, nonreflective finish.

Matte emulsion glaze Water-based; thins color; can be used as protective topcoat.

Metallic emulsion Water-based paint for decorative effects; available in tubs, pots, and spray form.

Silk emulsion Water-based vinyl or acrylic paint with a slight sheen; hardwearing, scuff-resistant, wipeable; available in matte (flat) and satin finishes.

Oil-based paint Includes wipeable gloss, satin, and eggshell (semi-matte) finishes. Use gloss for woodwork; satin and eggshell for walls or wood.

Primers Oil- or water-based paint used to seal unpainted surfaces to prevent covering coats of paint soaking in.

Satinwood Water-based paint finishes with a slight sheen.

Scumble glaze Thin top-coat of transparent print or an acrylic glaze combined with colorizers.

Silk emulsion Water-based vinyl or acrylic paint.

Specialist finishes Finishes formulated specifically for tricky areas, such as radiators, bathroom tiles, and fridges; examples include concrete melamine paint (for kitchen cupboards), and silicone paints (for metal surfaces), providing a smooth, hammered, heat-resistant finish.

Top coat Durable decorative surface.

Undercoat Usually oil-based, applied on top of the primer. It provides the right color base for the finishing coats, so should be the same color.

PAPER

Appliqué Cut-out design applied on top of another surface layer.

Block printing Pattern created by wood blocks that have had the pattern template carved onto them.

Embossed A raised design effect impressed onto wall covering by heat or pressure.

Flock Finely chopped fibers dropped onto pattern that has been printed in adhesive material to give a velvet appearance.

Grasscloth Grasses glued onto paper substrate.

Lining paper Plain paper that can be used to provide a surface for paint or for a top layer of wallpaper.

Prepasted Underside of wallpaper that has been treated with an adhesive which is then activated by water.

Run number A pattern and dye-lot number that appears on every roll. Choose rolls with the same number for a room.

Substrate Surface onto which the wall covering is applied.

TEXTILES

Boucle Knitted or woven fabric with looped knotted surface, made from rough, curly thread.

Canvas Tightly woven, durable cloth of rough texture, often used for utility items, typically made from cotton, acrylics, and blends treated to provide water resistance.

Cashmere Extremely soft and luxurious woolen fiber, made from the hair of the Kashmir goats of Tibet, Mongolia, China, Iran, Iraq, and India.

Chenille Thick, velvety cotton (as opposed to silk).

Damask Heavy cloth with a flat and reversible pattern woven into it (usually of same color), generally made of cotton, rayon, silk, or blends.

Felt Compact, non-woven fabric made from wool, hair and blends of synthetic fibres.

Fibre mix Silk with cotton, linen and viscose to change the properties of the material and hold its shape.

Fleece Stable pile fabric made from polyester. Warmer and lighter than wool, it dries rapidly and does not shrink or pull out of shape.

Jumbo cord Wide ribs of corduroy, usually made from cotton, with cut-pile weave.

Linens Formed from flax plant fibers they have a natural matte finish, that can be rustic and informal or elegant. Stronger than cotton, cool, easy to crease.

Lycra Synthetic fiber blends with cotton/wool/nylon. It has good stretch and recovery.

Mohair Soft woolen fabric made from the long hair of angora goats.

Muslin Plain woven sheer cotton.

Natural fibers Linen, cotton, silk, and wool.

Organzas A lightly textured, sheer fabric; often comprises contrasting layers, for example, matte and shine, transparency and translucency.

Neoprene Extremely durable, oil-resistant synthetic rubber.

Ripstock Lightweight breathable and tear resistant fabric. Can be coated to become waterproof, made with a heavier weave, or even have silver glass bead reflective surface applied to it for high visibility.

Silk Soft and lustrous natural fiber, typically created from cultivated worms, woven into a variety of weights.

Slubbed yarns Rough threads.

Synthetic fibers Artificial threads such as viscose, polyester, and acrylic. Often copies a natural product but with improved durability and water- and stain-resistant properties. Polyester and viscose content may have a slightly lower luster than those fused with silk, but it holds shape better.

Textured A presentation by which the textile is characterized: ruched, pleated, creased, crushed, smocked, or embossed.

Ticking Tighly woven durable fabric, typically cotton.

Tweed Medium- to heavy-weight woven material made from colored wool threads.

Upholstery fabric Hardwearing fabric designed to be durable, stain-resistant and flame-retardant.

Utility Durable fabrics such as denim, canvas, and hessian.

Velvet Luxurious medium-weight fabric with cut-pile soft furry surface.

Viscose Common type of rayon, a smooth material made from cellulose, similar to silk.

Yarn Cluster of threads twisted together to form a continuous strand, used in knitted or woven fabrics.

LEATHER

Aniline A delicate leather, finished to enhance the natural appearance of the hide. Usually dyed without additional color pigments and left without a protective coating. Aniline stains easily and permanently but acquires a pleasing patina.

Debossing A decorative finish, typically of machine-made uniformity or with specialist tools, that forms an indented mark on the surface of the leather.

Embossing A decorative finish, typically of machine-made uniformity or with specialist tools, that forms a raised mark on the surface of the leather.

Exotics Leathers such as crocodile, snake, lizard etc., generally available in smaller quantities than hides available as a by-product of the meat industry.

Finishing Numerous varieties of surface finish applied post-tanning. Used to give the hide its own unique look, conceal blemishes, modify surface colour and provide protection from wear. More finishing is required on lower-quality hides.

Grain The quality of the surface leather; determined by the condition and level of the surface damage and markings exposed once hair follicles are removed. Sometimes non-directional. The younger the animal, the finer the grain.

Hair-on-hide Hair follicles left on the skin to create the ultimate 'wild' look. Each hide is unique in colour and pattern.

Imitation leather Generally of consistent appearance, often made from vinyl, showing few of the natural blemishes and characteristics of real hide.

Laser-cut A machine process that cuts detailed and intricate patterns into the leather.

Leather A collective term for all hides and skins which have been tanned. A natural product, primarily sourced as a by-product of the meat industry—typically cow, sheep, goat, and pigskin. Fish leather and exotics such as crocodile, snake, lizard, etc. are also available in smaller quantities.

Nubuck An ultrafine sueded finish.

Patina A characteristic that builds up over time. This is not an applied finish.

Plated A special effect that enhances the natural grain of leather.

Tanning The process of stabilising and preserving the hide structure. Hides are sanitized, cleaned, and made into a consistent product.

Split Hides that are machine-cut into layers, and often shaved to form a skin of uniform thickness. The majority of hides are too thick for most applications so are typically "split."

Suede Soft, velvety look to the surface, predominantly formed from buffing a good-quality split.

WOOD

Antiqued/reclaimed Salvaged boards.

Bamboo Grass which over time takes on the characteristics of wood.

Bird's eye Wavy and circular formations in wood, resembling a bird's eye.

Blockboard Solid blocks of wood glued between veneers.

Bookmatching Sheets of wood veneer aligned to produce a symmetrical effect.

Cane Versatile and durable climbing palm, grown in the tropics and subtropics.

Chipboard Fragments of wood bonded with plastic glue.

Cork Derived from the bark of the evergreen cork tree (grown predominantly in Portugal); the bark is granulated, mixed with resins, pressed, and baked into tile or sheet form.

Hardboard Fragments of wood bonded by heat and pressure as opposed to glue and resin; usually has one smooth face and one rough face.

Hardwood Varied group of deciduous or evergreen trees grown in temperate and tropical areas.

Laminates Thin sheets of wood or veneer bonded onto substrate.

Limed/liming Softens the appearance of timber by lightening the grain.

MDF Medium-density fiberboard made up of particles of wood bonded with resin into a uniform board. Can be machined to good accuracy.

Marquetry/parquetry Thin inlay veneer.
Parquet Wood floors made from small blocks or strips, typically in geometric designs.

Plywood An odd number of thin layers of soft and hard woods glued together to form one piece of wood; most common is birch-faced ply.

Prefinished Oiled, waxed, or lacquered.

Softwood Fairly rapidly growing coniferous or needle-leaf trees typically grown in colder regions (North America, Canada, Russia, and Scandinavia); usually harvested after 60–80 years.

Staining Technique used to highlight the grain of the wood.

Veneer Thin slices of wood, producing subtle variations in grain and color; maximum leaf size is limited by the size of the log.

STONE

Antiqued/aged Stone which has been treated artificially to make it look older; processes to achieve this include acid washing, sand-/grit-blast, tumbling, and waxing.

Blending Technique designed to prevent obvious tonal differences in individual batches of stones; usually occurs prior to installation.

Bush-hammered A fairly rough cut; generally produces a light gray shade with white dots and an even surface with numerous markings, riddled in appearance; good nonslip qualities.

Chamfer Small bevel made on a corner.

Chiseled Manual or machine-cut, parallel and regular spaced grooves; variations in shade according to direction of grooves and light provide a contrast between treated/untreated areas.

Cleft See riven.

Flamed Mechanical technique where single or multiple jets of flame are directed onto a cooled section of sawn stone, after which the stone may be brushed to remove surface scales; thermal shock causes surface grains to shatter, giving the surface its slightly rough and irregular appearance.

Granite Very hard igneous rock.

Honed Smooth and uniform finish with a slight satin sheen, highlighting natural markings; created mechanically with a water-based finish by honing chains on large slice of sawn stone with smaller areas carried out by hand.

Limestone Sedimentary rock; often displays traces of shells and fossils.

Marble Metamorphic rock.

Polished Uniform surface, brilliant and highly reflective, with no visible scratching.

Quartzite Member of the sandstone family; extremely hard but tends to have a sugary appearance.

Riven Predominantly applied to slate, a traditional pitted finish that has been split rather than sawn; gives a lightly textured, even surface.

Sanded Semi-smooth, lightly abrasive, slip-resistant finish, similar to fine sandpaper.

Sand-/grit-blasting Treatment with a powerful jet of abrasive material (varied sizes of sand/metallic grit).

Sandstone Sedimentary rock with a high quartz content.

Sawn Technique for producing thin coverings, nominally ½ in. (1cm). Exterior applications not recommended for polished finishes.

Setts Small blocks of stone.

Slate Fine-grained metamorphic rock derived from clays and shale; it is formed from compressed layers of sediment under the ocean.

Split A fairly rough cut chiefly used for shaping rubble stones; presents the natural appearance of broken stone.

Striated A manual cut, produced from a split surface, resulting in continuous parallel lines.

Textured Flamed/bush-hammered/ sandblasted; a pitted or grooved finish; most commonly used for external paving, this technique provides strong contrast.

Traffic Measure of volume of use: light traffic—suitable for most residential use; medium traffic—suitable for use in all residential projects and light internal commercial applications; heavy traffic—suitable for a wide range of commercial applications.

Travertine Sedimentary rock; naturally pitted as the result of the presence of iron compounds or other organic impurities, and has a banded appearance from hot spring water penetrating through the limestone.

Tumbled When material is put into a rotating drum with pieces of gravel to blunt the edges, and expose pits, fossils, and veins.

Veining Color variations based on impurities present at formation in the original limestone rock.

CLAY

Ceramic Thin unit made from refined clay fired at high temperatures with an applied surface finish; can be glazed or unglazed.

Fully vitrified porcelain tiles Clay mixture is backed at 2336° F (1280° C); resilient to cracking and exposure to heat.

Flamed Rough stone-like finish.

Glazed Matte or gloss finish for tiles, which makes them resistant to water.

Grout Filler used to fill the gaps between tiles. Apply after adhesive has dried.

Incised Precision-cut tiles with lines scored into the surface.

Mosaic Small units typically mounted on a backing sheet.

Porcelain Dense clay that naturally has low porosity; tiles can be glazed or unglazed; glazed tiles have filled in microscopic holes that could be present in the unglazed tile.

Quarry tiles Unglazed tile made from unrefined natural clay or shale, burned at high temperature to produce a dense, strong tile that is low in porosity. Quarry tiles are usually red in color, of uniform texture and color, and do not gain patina with age.

Rectified edges Edges finished to match the surface; no trim required so edges can be exposed.

Terracotta Clay tiles.

Vitreous Like glass in structure and hardness; tiles are vitrified to make them less porous.

GLASS

Acid-etched/sandblasted Satin-smooth finish that obscures views and light; a permanent, soft, velvety finish.

Blocks Translucent units that diffuse and reflect light, and absorb sound and heat.

Color-laminated: Colored interlayer that produces single all-over color (opaque or transparent).

Enameled Durable, opaque finish, spray-painted or screen-printed onto a reverse surface and fused at high temperature; can be applied all over or in patterns ("frit").

Float glass Process of manufacture used to produce glass of uniform thickness; machine-cut to suit; can be toughened, laminated, acid-etched, screen-printed, beveled, decorated, or silvered.

Kilnforming Process that transforms ordinary flat glass into other shapes, textures, and patterns by heating and molding at high temperatures; most types of float glass ¼–1 in. (6–25mm) thick can be kilnformed (including toughened or laminated).

Laminated Safety glass formed from two or more sheets of glass with the resin interlayer (translucent or opaque) bonded at high pressure; the inner core holds fragments together if broken.

Low-e A form of thermal insulation to prevent excessive heat loss provided by a specialist coating that retains heat at night while allowing maximum daylight penetration; more appropriate to a cool climate.

Mirrored Chemically coated clear glass, often precision-shaped with polished or beveled edges; can be sandblasted and formed in large expanses or tiny mosaic; reflects light and gives increased sense of space.

Safety film Can be added to standard glass to prevent splintering if broken.

Screen-printed Colored enamel patterns are fired into the reverse side of the glass at high temperatures; gives sharp designs, smooth appearance, durability, and high levels of obscurity.

Textured Relief pattern formed into cast glass or by rolling a design onto a semi-molten surface; can be toughened or laminated.

Tinted glass Solar control properties that help reduce the amount of heat (and light) penetrating through into the interior by increasing the heat absorption of glass; transparent but with even color throughout it can be sandblasted or acid-etched.

Toughened Glass heated to high temperatures 1202°F (650°C) and then chilled rapidly, allowing outer and inner layers to cool at different rates and compressing the outer surfaces, resulting in increased strength; if shattered, breaks into tiny, harmless fragments.

Wired glass Increased fire resistance and security provided by fine steel mesh sandwiched between two layers of glass; if shattered, the fragments will not separate.

METALS

Alloy Metallic material comprising two or more metals or a mix of metal and non-metal.

Acid-etched Patterning technique producing a smooth matte finish.

Bead-blasted Lightly textured satin/matte finish.

Brushed Usually refers to stainless steel; matte finish.

Crimped Contrasting surface textures created in mesh by precision-bending.

Cable mesh Woven cable, formed into sheets.

Corrugated Molded steel sheets, usually coated with alumnium or zinc, or painted.

Enameled/coated High-gloss, high-color finish.

Embossed Textured decorative pattern on one surface.

Galvanized steel Steel coated with protective layer of zinc.

Perforated Pattern created by precision-cutting holes into a sheet.

Polished A shiny and reflective surface.

Satin/mill finish A shiny but less bright finish than that achieved by polishing.

DURABLES

Corian® A versatile trademarked product that blends natural minerals, pigments, and pure acrylic polymer to form a durable and seamless material.

Heat-seamed Joints are sealed with a welding rod to provide a continuous and impervious, wipe-clean, watertight finish.

Laminate Usually a chipboard base fused at high pressure with layers of paper impregnated with thermoplastic resin.

Linoleum Made from linseed oil, ground cork, wood flour, and resins, pressed onto a jute or hessian backing.

Quartzstone Composite product formed from natural aggregates, including quartz crystals, and acrylic resin to produce a high-performance, ultrasmooth surface.

Rubber flooring A processed natural product made from vulcanized synthetic rubber, silica, and pigment.

Technical stone High-performance reconstituted stone; comprises a concrete and natural minerals, sealed and highly polished to provide a nonporous surface.

Vinyl Synthetic product made from chlorinated petrochemicals; contains a proportion of PVC, the amount of which is in direct proportion to quality and performance. Vinyl flooring is typically made of several layers with a printed image sandwiched between a clear vinyl layer and a felt or vinyl backing.

SITE SURFACES

Aggregate Granular mixture of sand, coarser stones, and gravel; used to form mortar or concrete.

Cement Limestone and aluminous clay, gypsum, and sand.

Concrete Hard building material made from cement, sand, small stones, and water.

Curing Time period during which surfaces are left to harden; there must be an even temperature to work and cure the substance without cracking, usually within 50–86°F (10–30°C).

Granulated finish Natural and synthetic aggregates and stones are bound with clear epoxy resin.

In situ Created on-site, as opposed to prefabricated off-site.

Plaster A combination of powdered and heat-treated gypsum, which can be mixed with water to create a paste; it needs no heat to mature and hardens to a smooth solid which does not shrink or lose volume.

Resin Binding agent (clear or colored). A self-leveling topping onto screed,

Scagliola Imitation stone, such as marble, formed by mixing finely ground gypsum with glue and splinters of stone.

Screed Sand and cement subfloor to concrete, with surface finish.

Stone carpet Blend of naturally occurring aggregates and stone particles encapsulated in clear resin.

Stucco Smooth rendering made from cement, sand, and lime; applied while soft to cover exterior walls or surfaces.

Substrate Surface onto which the top surface is laid.

Terrazzo Cement- or resin-based material embedded with chips of glass, marble, and/or granite; poured into place and then ground or polished into a smooth surface.

Troweled Smooth or uniform concrete or plaster surface obtained by using a trowel.

Supplier Information

1. Abbott & Boyd
www.abbottandboyd.co.uk

Tel: +44 (0)20 7351 9985
Fax: +44 (0)20 7823 3127

2. Alma Home
www.almahome.co.uk

Tel: +44 (0)20 7377 0762
Fax: +44 (0)20 7375 2471

3. Alternative Flooring Company
www.alternativeflooring.com

Tel: +44 (0)1264 335111
Fax: +44 (0)1264 336445
Email:
sales@alternativeflooring.com

4. Altro
www.altrofloors.com

US
Tel: +1 650 941 1696
Fax:+1 650 941 2961
Email: west@altrofloors.com

UK
Altro Limited
www.altro.co.uk

Tel: +44 (0)1462 480480
Email: info@altro.co.uk

5. Amron Associates Ltd.
www.amronassociates.co.uk

Tel: +44 (0)1302 533111
Fax: +44 (0)1302 536722
Email:
info@amronassociates.co.uk

6. Amtico
www.amtico.com

US
Tel: +1 404 267 1900
Fax: +1 404 267 1901

UK
Tel: +44 (0)870 350 4080
Fax: +44 (0)870 350 4081

7. Anaglypta
www.anaglypta.co.uk

US Distributor
The Imperial Home Decor Group
Tel: +1 216 378 5200
Fax: +1 216 378 5599

UK
Anaglypta
Tel: +44 (0)1254 222800

8. Anita Lear
Tel: +44 (0)1597 825505
Email: lear@marquetry.co.uk

9. Anne Kyyro Quinn
www.annekyyroquinn.com

Tel: +44 (0)20 7021 0702
Fax: +44 (0)20 7021 0770
Email: info@anneKyyroquinn.com

10. Area Rugs and Carpets
www.arearugs.co.uk

Tel: +44 (0)1924 519243
Email:
andrew.warburton@arearugs.co.uk

11. Armourcoat Surface Finishes

US
www.armourcoatusa.com
Tel: +1 402 896 2005
Fax: +1 402 895 7238

UK
www.armourcoat.com
Tel: +44 (0)1732 460668
Fax: +44 (0)1732 450930
Email: sales@armourcoat.co.uk
technical@armourcoat.co.uk

12. Armstrong World Industries
www.armstrong.com

Tel: +44 (0)1642 768600
Fax: +44 (0)1642 750006

13. Artex-Rawlplug
www.bpb.co.uk

Tel: +44 (0)115 945 6100
Fax: +44 (0)115 945 6041
Email: info@bpb.com

14. Atrium
Tel: +44 (0)20 7379 7288
Fax: +44 (0)20 7240 2080

15. B. Brown
Tel: +44 (0)8705 117118
Fax: +44 (0)8705 329020

16. Bill Amberg
www.billamberg.com

Tel: +44 (0)20 7727 3560
Fax: +44 (0)20 7727 3541

17. Bisazza Mosaico
www.bisazzausa.com

US
Tel: +1 305 597 4099
Fax: +1 305 597 9844
Email: info@bisazzausa.com
Tel: +1 212 334 7130
Fax: +1 212 334 7131
Email: infony@bisazzausa.com

UK
Tel: +44 (0)20 8640 7994
Fax: +44 (0)20 8640 5664
Email: info@bisazza.com

18. Bollom
www.bollom.com

Tel: +44 (0)20 8658 2299

19. Brian Yates
www.brian-yates.co.uk

Tel: +44 (0)1524 35035
Email: sales@brian-yates.co.uk

20. Brintons Carpets
www.brintons.net

US
Tel: +1 212 832 0121
Email:
commercialinfo@brintonsusax.com

UK
Tel: +44 (0)1562 820000

21. Bristol (UK) Limited
www.bristolpaint.com

Tel: +44 (0)20 7624 4370
Email: tech.sales@bristolpaint.com

22. Brundle
www.fhbrundle.com

Tel: +44 (0)20 8525 7100

23. Bruno Triplet
Tel: +44 (0)20 7823 9990

24. Burlington Stone
www.burlingtonstone.co.uk

US
Tel: +1 972 985 9182
Fax: +1 972 612 0847
Email: BURSTONE@prodigy.net

UK
Burlington Slate Limited
Tel: +44 (0)1229 889 661
Fax: +44 (0)1229 889 466
Email:
enquires@burlingtonstone.co.uk

25. Capital Marble Design
www.capitalmarble.co.uk

Tel: +44 (0)20 8968 5340

26. Cellbond Composites
www.cellbond.com

US
Tel: +1 218 532 2012
Email: sales.usa@cellbond.com

UK
Tel: +44 (0)1480 435302
Fax: +44 (0)1480 450181
Email: sales@cellbond.com

27. Cole & Son Ltd.
www.cole-and-son.com

US Distributor
Lee Jofa Inc.
Tel: +1 516 752 7600

UK
Tel: +44 (0)20 8442 8844
Fax: +44 (0)20 8802 0033
Email:
customer.service@cole-and-son.com

28. Concrete Information Ltd
www.concreteinfo.org

Tel: +44 (0)1276 608 770
Fax: +44 (0)1276 373 69
Email: enquiries@concreteinfo.org

29. DuPont Corian/DuPont Zodiaq
www.corian.com

Tel: +44 (0)1442 218 500
Email: info@dupont.com

30. Crucial Trading
www.crucial-trading.com

Tel: +44 (0)1562 743 747

31. Dalsouple
www.dalsouple.com

Tel: +44 (0)1278 727 733
Fax: +44 (0)1278 727 766
Email: info@dalsouple.com

32. Degussa

US
www.degussa.com
Tel: +1 973 541 80 00
Fax: +1 973 541 80 13

UK
www.degussa-cc.co.uk
Tel: +44 (0)161 794 7411
Fax: +44 (0)161 727 8547
E-mail: mbtfeb@degussa.com

33. Designers Guild
www.designersguild.com

Tel: + 44 (0)20 7893 7400
Fax:+44 (0)20 7893 7720
Email: info@designersguild.co.uk

34. Desso DLW Sports Systems
www.dessodlw.com

Tel: +44 (0)1494 680 088
Fax +44 (0)1494 680 020
Email: info@ddsports.com

35. Dominic Crinson
www.crinson.com
www.digitile.co.uk

Tel: +44 (0)20 7613 2783

36. Domus Tiles
www.domustiles.com

Tel: +44 (0)20 7091 1500
Fax: +44 (0)20 7091 1501
Email: service@domustiles.com

37. Donghia
www.donghia.com

US
Tel: +1 212 925 2777
Fax: +1 212 925 4819
Email: mail@donghia.com

UK
Tel: +44 (0)20 7823 3456
Fax: +44 (0)20 7376 5758
Email: sales@donghia.uk.com

38. Easi Fall International Ltd.
www.easifall.co.uk

Tel: +44 (0)1619 730304
Fax: +44 (0)1619 695009
Email: enquiries@easifall.com

39. Easifloor Ltd.
www.easifloor.co.uk

Tel: +44 (0)1268 288744
Fax: +44 (0)1268 532305
Email: info@easifloor.co.uk

40. Ecoimpact Ltd.
www.ecoimpact.co.uk

Tel: +44 (0)20 8940 7072
Fax: +44 (0)20 8332 1218

41. Ecos Organic Paints
www.ecospaints.com

Tel: +44 (0)1524 852371
Fax: +44 (0)1524 858978
Email: mail@ecospaints.com

42. Expanko Inc.
www.expanko.com

Tel: +1 800 345 6202
Fax: +1 610 593 3027
Email: sales@expanko.com

43. Fired Earth
www.firedearth.com

Tel: +44 (0)1295 812088
Fax: +44 (0)1295 810832
Email: enquiries@firedearth.com

44. Floor Source
www.floorsourceuk.com

Tel: +44 (0)1216 355 770
Fax: +44 (0)1216 355 771

45. Floor Co.
Tel: +44 (0)1933 418899

46. Forbo Flooring

US
www.forbo-industries.com
Tel: +1 570 459 0771
Fax: +1 570 450 0258

UK
www.forbo-flooring.co.uk
Tel: +44 (0)1592 643 777
Fax: +44 (0)1592 643 999

47. Formica

US
www.formica.com
Tel: +1 513 744 8700
Fax: +1 513 744 8749

UK
www.formica.co.uk
Tel: +44 (0)191 259 3000
Fax: +44 (0)191 258 2719
Email: formica.limited@formica.co.uk

48. Fox Linton
www.foxlinton.com

Tel: +44 (0)20 7501 7700
Email: info@foxlinton.com

49. Francesca Di Blasi Co Ltd.
Tel: +44 (0)20 7938 2244
Fax: +44 (0)20 7938 1920
Email: info@thecube.com

50. Fritz Industries
www.fritztile.com

Tel: +1 972 285 5471
Fax: +1 972 270 0179
Email: tilesales@fritzind.com

51. Fusion Glass Designs Ltd.
www.fusionglass.co.uk

Tel: +44 (0)20 7738 5888
Fax: +44 (0)20 7738 4888

52. GKD

US
www.gkdusa.com
Tel: +1 410 221 0542
Fax:+1 410 221 0544
Email: sales@gkdusa.com

UK
www.creativeweave.com/engl/index
Tel: +44 (0)1977 686410
Fax: +44 (0)1977 686411
Email: sales@gkd.uk.com

53. Glass Block Technology Ltd.
www.glassblocks.co.uk

Tel: +44 (0)161 612 6893
Fax: +44 (0)161 285 1503
Email: info@glassblocks.co.uk

54. Glaverbel
www.glaverbel.com

US
Crystal International
Tel: +1 201 227 9095, 6, 7, 8
Fax: +1 201 227 2500
Email: crystal@crystalnewyork.com

UK
Glaverbel
Tel: + 44 (0)1788 535353
Fax: + 44(0)1788 560853
Email: gvb.uk@glaverbel.com

55. Gooding Aluminium Ltd.
www.goodingalum.com

Tel: +44 (0)20 8692 2255
Fax: +44 (0)20 8469 0031
Email: sales@goodingalum.com

56. Graham & Brown Ltd.
www.grahambrown.com

US
Tel: +1 609 395 9200
Fax: +1 609 395 9676
Email:
pspringman@grahambrownusa.com

UK
Tel: +44 (0)1254 691 321
Fax: +44 (0)1254 696 137

57. Green Bottle Unit
www.green-bottle.co.uk

Tel: +44 (0)20 7249 3394
Fax: +44 (0)20 7249 8499
Email: contact@green-bottle.co.uk

58. H & R Johnson Tiles Ltd.
www.johnson-tiles.com

Tel: +44 (0)1782 575 575
Fax: +44 (0)1782 577 377

59. Hammerite
www.hammerite.com

Tel: +44 (0)1661 830 000
Fax: +44 (0)1661 838 200

60. Harvey Maria Ltd.
www.harveymaria.co.uk

Tel: +44 (0)20 8542 0088
Fax: +44 (0)20 8542 0099
Email: info@harveymaria.co.uk

61. Helen Sheane Ltd.
www.helensheanewallcoverings.
co.uk

Tel: +44 (0)1295 273 644
Fax: +44 (0)1295 273 646

62. Helen Yardley
www.helenyardley.com

Tel: +44 (0)20 7253 9242
Fax: +44 (0)20 7403 8906
Email: gallery@helenyardley.com

63. Hornitex Ltd.
www.hornitex.com
Tel: +44 (0)1482 644671
Fax: +44 (0)1405 601006
Email: info.uk@hornitex.com

64. H & B Wire Fabrications Ltd.
www.hbwf.co.uk

Tel: +44 (0)1925 819 515
Fax: +44 (0)1925 831 773

65. Ian Mankin Fabrics
Tel: +44 (0)20 7722 0997

66. Ibstock Brick
www.ibstock.co.uk

Tel: +44 (0)1530 261999
Fax: +44 (0)1530 257457

67. Island Stone
www.islandstone.co.uk

Tel: +44 (0)800 083 9351
Fax: +44 (0)800 083 9352
Email: sales@islandstone.co.uk

68. Isocrete Commercial Flooring
www.isocrete.co.uk

Tel: +44 (0)1270 753000
Fax: +44 (0)1270 753333
Email: help@isocrete.com

69. Jaymart Rubber & Plastics Ltd.
www.jaymart.net

Tel: +44 (0)1373 864926
Fax: +44 (0)1373 858454
Email: matting@jaymart.net

70. Junckers Hardwood
www.junckershardwood.com

Tel: +44 (0)1376 517512
Fax: +44 (0)1376 514401

71. Kasthall
www.kasthall.com

US
Tel: +1 212 421 0220
Fax: +1 212 421 0230
Email:
manuela.scilironi@kasthall.se

UK
Kasthall Agent: Sinclair Till
Tel: +44 (0)20 7720 0031
Fax: +44 (0)20 7498 3814
Email: sinclairtill@lineone.net

72. Kirkstone
www.kirkstone.com

Tel: +44 (0)1539 433296
Email: info@kirkstone.com

73. Klober Ltd.
www.klober.co.uk

Tel: +44 (0)1509 650650
Fax: +44 (0)1509 600061
Email: support@klober.co.uk

74. KM Europa Metal AG

US
ww.kmeamerica.com
Tel: +1 630 990 2025
Fax: +1 630 990 0258
Email: sales@kmeamerica.com

UK
www.kme-uk.com
Tel: +44 (0)1905 751800
Fax: +44 (0)1905 751801
Email: info-uk@kme.com

75. Kvadrat Ltd.
www.kvadrat.dk

US Distributor
Maharam
www.maharam.com

Tel: +1 800 645 3943
Fax: +1 631 582 1026

UK
Tel: +44 (0)20 7229 9969
Fax: +44 (0)20 7229 1543
Email: uk@kvadrat.org

76. Lassco Flooring
www.lassco.co.uk

Tel: +44 (0)20 7394 2101
Fax: +44 (0)20 7394 2131
Email: flooring@lassco.co.uk

77. Lucite International

US
www.luciteusa.com
Tel: +1 901 381 2000
Fax: +1 901 381 2447

UK
www.luciteinternational.com
Tel: +44 (0)870 240 4620
Fax: +44 (0)870 240 4626
Email: contactus@lucite.com

78. M.I.D Carpets
www.mid.nl

US
Tel: +1 800 222 9005
Fax: +1 770 382 4986
Email: info@vandijkcarpet.com

UK
Bill Nunn Manufacturers Agent
Tel: +44 (0)1992 642753
Email: bill.nunn@btinternet.com

79. Marley Floors
www.marleyfloors.com

US Distributors:
Commercial Flooring
Tel: +1 407 788 5331
Email: cfdflooring@aol.com

Floor Supply Distributing
Tel: +1 509 535 9707
Email:
floorsupply@worldnet.att.net

UK
Tel: +44 (0)1622 854 040
Fax: +44 (0)1622 854 520
Email: info@marley.com

80. Marvick Textiles
www.marvictextiles.co.uk

US
Email:
sales.usa@marvictextiles.co.uk

UK
Sales: +44 (0)20 8993 0191
Fax: +44 (0)20 8993 1484
Email: sales@marvictextiles.co.uk

**81. MASS—Cast Advanced
Concretes**
www.castadvancedconcretes.com

Tel: +44 (0)1929 480757
Fax: +44 (0)1929 481695
Email:
info@castadvancedconcretes.com

82. Melin Tregwynt
www.melintregwynt.co.uk

Tel: +44 (0)1348 891225
Email: info@melintregwynt.co.uk

83. Milliken Carpet
www.millikencarpet.com

US
Tel: +1 800 257 3987

UK
Tel: +44 (0)1942 826073

84. Muskett Mazzullo
www.muskett-mazzullo.co.uk

Tel: +44 (0)20 7354 5976
Fax: +44 (0)20 7354 5696
Email:
nicole@muskett-mazzullo.co.uk

85. Natural Elements Ltd.
www.natural-elements.co.uk

Tel: +44 (0)207 354 8100
Fax: +44 (0)207 354 9977
Email:
sales@natural-elements.co.uk

86. The Natural Tile Company
www.naturaltile.co.uk

Tel: +44 (0)1285 642314
Fax: +44 (0)1285 642324
Email: sales@naturaltile.co.uk

87. Nielsen McNally
www.simply-scandinavian.co.uk

Tel: +44 (0)1252 326 416
Fax: +44 (0)1252 334 490
E-mail: Birte.Nielsen@nielsen-mcnally.co.uk

88. Nippon Electric Glass
www.neg.co.jp/eng

US
Tel: +1 630 285 8500
Fax: +1 630 285 8510

UK
Tel: +44 (0)2920 498747
Fax: +44 (0)2920 490487

89. Opals (Mirror-Flex) Co. Ltd.
www.mirrorflex.co.uk

Tel: +44 (0)1255 423 927
Fax: +44 (0)1255 221 117
Email info@mirrorflex.co.uk

90. Osborne & Little
www.osborneandlittle.com

Tel: +44 (0)20 7352 1456
Fax: +44 (0)20 7351 7813
Email:
showroom@osborneandlittle.com

91. Paper & Paint Library
www.paintlibrary.co.uk

Tel: +44 (0)20 7581 1075
Fax: +44 (0)20 7590 9860
Email: paintlibrary@fastnet.co.uk

92. Paper Moon
www.papermoon.co.uk

Tel: +44 (0)1438 880800
Fax: +44 (0)1438 880700
Email: info@papermoon.co.uk

93. Paragon Glass Designs Ltd.
www.paragonglass.co.uk

Tel: +44 (0)20 8507 2455
Fax: +44 (0)20 8507 2457
Email: info@paragonglass.co.uk

94. Paris Ceramics
www.parisceramics.com

US
Tel: +1 212 644 2782
Email:
newyork@parisceramics.com
Tel: +1 323 658 8570
Email:
losangeles@parisceramics.com

UK
Tel: +44 (0)20 7371 7778

95. Patagonia
www.patagonia.com

US
Tel: +1 800 638 6464
Fax: +1 800 543 5522

Europe
Tel: +33 (0)450 884444
Fax +33 (0)450 884499
Email:
euro.customer.sce@Patagonia.com

96. Pergo
www.pergo.com

US
Tel: +1 919 773 6000
Fax: +1 919 773 6004
Email: casupport@pergo.com

UK
Tel: +44 (0)1235 556 300
Fax: +44 (0)1235 556 350
Email: info@pergo.com

97. Pilkington
www.pilkington.com

US
Tel: +1 419 247 3731
Fax: +1 419 247 3821

UK
Tel: +44 (0)20 7747 6000
Fax: +44 (0)20 7747 6009

98. Polartec
www.polartec.com

Email: polartec@maldenmills.com

99. Potter & Soar Ltd.
www.wiremesh.co.uk

Tel: +44 (0)1295 253344
Fax: +44 (0)1295 272132
Email:
Potter.Soar@btinternet.com

100. Rachel Kelly
www.interactivewallpaper.co.uk

Tel: +44 (0)20 7490 3076
Email:
studio@interactivewallpaper.co.uk

101. Rimex Group
www.rimexmetals.com

US
Tel: +1 732 549 3800
Fax: +1 732 549 6435
Email: sales@rimexusa.com

UK
Tel: +44 (0)20 8804 0633
Fax: +44 (0)20 8804 7275
Email: sales@rimexmetals.com

102. Roger Oates
www.rogeroates.com

Tel: +44 (0)1531 631611

103. Ruckstuhl
www.ruckstuhl.com

104. Rupert Scott
www.rupertscott.com

Tel: +44 (0)1743 851393
Fax: +44 (0)1743 851393
Email: info@rupertscott.com

105. Ruth Spaak Glass

Tel: +44 (0)1789 415244
Email: ruthspaak@hotmail.com

106. Saint Gobain
www.saint-gobain-glass.com

US
Tel: +1 480 607 9400
Fax: +1 480 607 94 06

UK
Tel: +44 (0)1977 666100
Fax: +44 (0)1977 666200
Email:
sgguk@saint-gobain-glass.com

107. Saldo
www.saldo.com

Tel: +46 (0)44 126 181
Fax:+46 (0)44 126 182
E-mail: mailbox@saldo.com

108. Santos & Adolfsdottir
Tel: +44 (0)1722 714669

109. Shadbolt International
www.shadbolt.co.uk

Tel: +44 (0)20 8527 6441
Fax: +44 (0)20 8523 2774
Email: sales@shadbolt.co.uk

110. Siesta Cork Tile Co.
www.siestacorktiles.co.uk

Tel: +44 (0)20 8683 4055
Fax: +44 (0)20 8683 4480

111. Smile Plastics Ltd.
www.smileplastics.co.uk

Tel: +44 (0)1743 850267
Fax: +44 (0)1743 851067
Email: SmilePlas@aol.com

112. Solid Floor Ltd.
www.solidfloor.co.uk

Tel: +44 (0)20 7221 9166
Email: nottinghill@solidfloor.co.uk

113. Spinneybeck
www.spinneybeck.com

US
Tel: +1 716 446 2380
Fax: +1 716 446 2396
Email: sales@spinneybeck.com

114. Stepan Tertsakian Ltd.
www.stertsakiansheepskins.co.uk

Tel: +44 (0)20 7236 8788
Email:
john@stertsakiansheepskins.co.uk

115. Stone Age Ltd.
www.estone.co.uk
Tel: +44 (0)20 7384 9090
Fax: +44 (0)20 7384 9099
Email: info@estone.co.uk

116. Stonell Ltd.
www.stonell.com

Tel: +44 (0)20 7738 0606
Fax: +44 (0)20 7738 0660

117. Strata Tiles
Tel: +44 (0)1252 890434

118. Swarovski Crystal
www.swarovski.com

US
Tel: +1 800 426 3088
Fax: +1 800 870 5660
Email: customer_relations.us@
swarovski.com

UK
Tel: +44 (0)1737 856814
Fax: +44 (0)1737 856856
Email: customer_relations.gb@
swarovski.com

119. Tileco Ltd.
www.tileco.co.uk

Tel: +44 (0)20 8481 9500
Fax: +44 (0)20 8481 9501
Email: info@tileco.co.uk

120. Timorous Beasties
www.timorousbeasties.com

Tel: +44 (0)141 959 3331
Fax: +44 (0)141 959 8880

121. Top Floor Rugs
www.topfloorrugs.com

Tel: +44 (0)20 7795 3333
Fax: +44 (0)20 7351 5419
Email: info@topfloorrugs.com

122. Tretford Carpets
www.tretford.ie

US Distributor
Eurotex Inc.
Tel: +1 800 523 0731
Fax: +1 215 423 0940

UK/Eire
Tel: +353 51 375 941
Fax: +353 51 379 607
Email: enquiries@tretford.ie

123. Tyndale Carpets
www.tyndalecarpets.com

Tel: +44 (0)20 7473 8888
Fax: +44 (0)20 7473 8890
Email: sales@tyndalecarpets.com

124. Ulf Moritz

US Distributor
www.bergamofabrics.com
Tel: +1 914 665 0800
Email: rachel@bergamofabrics.com

UK Distributor
www.brian-yates.co.uk
Tel: +44 (0)1524 35035
Email: sales@brian-yates.co.uk

125. Veedon Fleece Ltd.
www.veedonfleece.com

Tel: +44 (0)1483 575758
Fax: +44 (0)1483 535790
Email: veedon@veedonfleece.com

126. Winther Browne
www.wintherbrowne.co.uk

Tel: +44 (0)20 8884 6000
Fax: +44 (0)20 8884 6001
Email: sales@wintherbrowne.co.uk

127. Woods of Wales
Tel: +44 (0)1938 554789
Fax: +44 (0)1938 554921

128. Wool Classics
Tel: +44 (0)20 7349 0090
Fax: +44 (0)20 7349 0035
Email: showrooms@chdc.co.uk

129. World's End Tiles Ltd.
www.worldsendtiles.co.uk

Tel: +44 (0)20 7819 2110
Fax: +44 (0)30 7819 2101
Email:
showroom@worldsendtiles.co.uk

130. Zinc Counters
www.zinccounters.co.uk

Tel: +44 (0)1765 677808
Fax: +44 (0)1765 677808
Email: sales@zinccounters.co.uk

131. Check your local suppliers.

132. Paint effects can be created
with many types of paint, which
you can find locally. For ideas try:

The Paint Effects Bible by Kerry
Skinner (Firefly Books, 2003)
The Paint Effects Manual by Kerry
Skinner (Apple Press, 2003)

Index

Credits

Quarto would like to thank and acknowledge the following for supplying photographs reproduced in this book:

p2 Jan Baldwin / Narratives
p6 Jan Baldwin / Narratives
p10 M.I.D. Carpets
p14 M.I.D. Carpets w
p20 Crucial Trading
p26 Stephen J. Whitehorne / Myriad Images
p28 Roger Oates Design
p48 Graham & Brown Stockists:
p52 From the "Oasis" wallcovering collection by Brian Yates
p56 Deborah Bowness. Digital and hand silkscreen printed on paper – with genuine fake bookshelf. Soho house LONDON
p62 Eleanor Pritchard www.eleanorpritchard.com
p66 Jan Baldwin / Narratives
p70 Jan Baldwin / Narratives
p72 Osborne and Little
p78 Osborne and Little
p82 Osborne and Little
p86 David Koppel / Alma
p90 Top Floor UK Ltd
p92 David Koppel / Alma
p94 David Koppel / Alma
p100 Eclectics www.eclectics.co.uk
p102 Tamsyn Hill / Narratives
p104 Jan Baldwin / Narratives
p110 Fired Earth
p112 Fired Earth
p114 Armstrong World Industries
p116 Jan Baldwin / Narratives
p118 Armstrong World Industries
p120 Crucial Trading
p122 Lynn Donaldson Photography / Expanko Inc.
p124 Island Stone
p128 Kirkstone
p132 Kirkstone
p136 Fired Earth
p140 Kirkstone

p142 Jan Baldwin / Narratives
p148 Fired Earth
p154 Surface Tiles www.surfacetiles.com
p158 Fired Earth
p160 Peter Dixon / Narratives
p166 Saint-Gobain Glass
p170 Jan Baldwin / Narratives
p172 Fired Earth
p182 Jan Baldwin / Narratives
p186 Jan Baldwin / Narratives
p188 HBWF Limited and Amron Associates Limited
p196 Christopher Everard / Dalsouple
p200 From the PLAY Collection by SCIN, kitchen cupboard doors in 5mm Opal Perspex and splashback in 5mm Blue Frosted Perspex www.scin.co.uk
p204 The Amtico Company
p206 Du Pont® from the Zen Vanity collection by CORIAN®: Nocturne, Bone, Italy, design: Massimo Fucci
p212 Jan Baldwin / Narratives
p214 Jan Baldwin / Narratives
p218 Jan Baldwin / Narratives
p220 Surface Tiles www.surfacetiles.com
p222 M.I.D. Carpets
p237 Saint-Gobain Glass

All other photographs and illustrations are the copyright of Quarto Inc. While every effort has been made to credit contributors, Quarto would like to apologize should there have been any omissions or errors—and would be pleased to make the appropriate correction for future editions of the book.

The author would like to thank Annette Main for her invaluable assistance.